# MICKEY ROURKE
## High And Low

**Christopher Heard**

Plexus, London

For Isabelle . . . and absinthe

British Library Cataloguing in Publication Data

Heard, Christopher
  Mickey Rourke : high and low
  1. Rourke, Mickey 2. Motion picture actors and
  actresses -
  United States - Biography
  I. Title
  791.4'3'028'092

  ISBN-10: 0-85965-386-2
  ISBN-13: 978-0-85965-386-2

Printed and bound in Great Britain by Cromwell Press
Book and cover design by Rebecca Longworth

Acknowledgements
First and foremost, I would like to thank Mickey Rourke for
his time and for his story.
   Thanks to Sandra Wake, Julia Shone, and the rest of the
good folks at Plexus for getting behind this project early. It
has been a pleasure working with you. Thanks to Paul
Woods. A good editor makes all the difference in the world.
Thanks to my family: Marie, Bill, and my brother and great
friend Peter. Thanks to Betty for her love and encourage-
ment. Without it none of it would mean anything at all.
Thanks to Chris Alexander (the Annihilator) – a good friend
who spurred me on constantly, if for no other reason than he
wanted to read the book. Very special thanks to Heather and
uniquelyrourke.com – a special friend and a great resource.
Thanks also to Stephy of uniquelyrourke.com. Thanks to
Martha Fusca – a great boss and an even better friend.
Thanks to Anna Fuci – my friend and protector. Thanks to all
my iChannel family: Victoria Fusca, Rosemary Fusca, Myra
Dziama, Angie Dawson, Frank Bertolas, and Paul Yedema.

# CONTENTS

# PREFACE

'How many whose praises used once to be sung so loudly are now relegated to oblivion; and how many singers themselves have long since passed from sight!' – *Marcus Aurelius*

I have always been a fan of Mickey Rourke's work. I can track it back to a specific afternoon in downtown Toronto, Canada in late August of 1981. I was sixteen years old and running an errand for my grandmother; she was a hairdresser and needed me to pick up some supplies at a beauty shop supply outlet. I was anxious to grab the stuff and then slip into the old Imperial 6 theatre, to catch the first afternoon showing of the newly released film *Body Heat*, William Hurt's foray into *film noir*.

I had always loved movies, being a kind of junior film historian ever since I was a small child. As a kid, I would stay up all night after studying the TV listings, looking for anything directed by John Huston or Howard Hawks or Billy Wilder. So when *Body Heat* arrived amidst a stir of controversy over its sexual explicitness and supposed moral bankruptcy, I was eager to see what all the fuss was about. But what intrigued me most was the suggestion that it was starkly original. Even at my relatively young age, I had a feeling that originality in Hollywood was strictly a thing of the past – and from what I had been reading about the plot of *Body Heat*, it sounded a whole lot like *Double Indemnity* to me.

Once in the theatre, I found myself enjoying the film. It was quite risqué for the time, and William Hurt and Kathleen Turner lived up to the hype. But when Mickey Rourke appeared, in his small role as the arsonist Teddy Lewis, he blew Hurt right off the screen. At that moment I instantly became a fan of Rourke's, and eagerly followed whatever he did from that point on.

Now let's jump ahead twenty years. The location is still Toronto, about ten blocks north and three blocks west of where the Imperial 6 theatre once stood. I am sitting on the sun-soaked balcony of a suite in the Four Seasons Hotel, and Mickey Rourke is sitting opposite me. I've now been on TV for twelve years as a movie reviewer and interviewer, have written books about movies and cinema journalism for publications such as *Movieline, ELLE* and a terrific Canadian lifestyle magazine called *Dolce Vita*. On this day the Toronto International Film Festival is in full swing, and Rourke is in attendance to promote his film *Spun*.

Rourke looked tired that day. He had been enjoying his time in Toronto (as the gossip columns testified) and was a bit weary. I had been following his career with keen interest for a long time, so I was well aware of his ups and downs, highs and lows. But I didn't want to be just another scribbling asshole making verbal gibes, as so many had done of late. I considered myself lucky to be in the presence of a guy with such proven talent and personal eccentricity.

*The kind of figure that just doesn't come out of Hollywood anymore: Mickey Rourke with the author, during the 2002 Toronto International Film Festival.*

As I joined Rourke on the balcony, we exchanged handshakes and pleasantries. I told him that I was a big fan of his work. 'Hey, thanks man,' came his response. He sounded sincere. I laid a folded newspaper on the glass table where we sat, with an item about Rourke and his alleged behaviour the night before at an aptly named Toronto nightspot called the Bovine Sex Club. He noted it and looked at me with a smirk.

'So what do you want to talk about?' asked Rourke, already starting to turn cynical.

'Just out of curiosity, why do you think no one went to *Johnny Handsome*?' I asked. 'I thought that it was one of the truly underrated films of the Eighties.' Rourke lit a cigarette, glanced down to check on the little sleeping Chihuahua at his feet, and leaned forward. 'Well, I'll tell ya. Walter Hill has a great talent for writing, but he tried to do too many things with that movie, tell too many different stories about too many different things that didn't belong in the same movie . . .' Two hours plus later, I left Mickey Rourke's hotel suite. He'd given me one of the most enjoyable interviews I'd ever conducted.

I was originally intending to call that magazine piece 'Mickey High and Low', as I liked the sound of the title. But then I scratched in my notebook, 'Change title – *Mickey High and Low* is what I will call the book.'

It was on that day that the seeds of this book were sown. Ever since then, Rourke has continually reaffirmed his status as a great re-emergent talent. With the release of *Killshot*, he has finally got himself to the place he was heading toward before his career crashed and burned. From hereon in, he gets to do interesting work that he doesn't have to be ashamed of; filmmakers need not be afraid of his manufactured reputation, the way they seemed to be during his period of exile. And he no longer has the pressure of being the guy who failed to live up to the glorious potential he initially displayed. So now is the perfect time to tell his inspiring story. Rourke is unique in that he has always lived the way he wanted to – a characteristic that has led him to the highest of highs and dropped him to the lowest of lows. But, despite whatever is written by critics or gossip hawkers, Mickey Rourke is no asshole. He was described to me as a loyal friend, and 'a sweet, soft spoken, sensitive guy', by all who know him and have worked with him, from Francis Ford Coppola to Daryl Hannah. He is an actor who makes instinctual choices both in his professional life and in his personal life, both enjoying and suffering the consequences with few regrets.

He's still taking risks, rocking boats, disturbing shit – just being Mickey Rourke. He's simply not the kind of figure we are used to coming out of Hollywood lately.

*Rourke as a 1980s icon, complete with designer stubble: as Harold Angel in* Angel Heart *(1987).*

# Chapter One

# MIAMI VIA SCHENECTADY

## 'I would have liked to have come from somewhere normal, somewhere simple.' – *Mickey Rourke*

Mickey Rourke was born Philip Andre Rourke Jr. in Schenectady, New York, on a warm Indian summer's day, 16 September, 1956. Although, depending on who you ask or what your sources are, the date could have been 1950 or 1953. But, for the sake of this biography, I am going with the year that Rourke himself told me.

Schenectady is one of those small cities in upstate New York that people in New York City itself joke about. Rourke's father, Philip Sr., worked as a groundskeeper and janitor at a golf and country club. He spent his off-hours lifting weights and working out, and had a well developed, chiselled physique that Mickey would grow up trying to emulate. The Rourkes' Irish background (their ancestors migrated from County Cork), and the fact that Philip Sr. was an avid New York Yankees/Mickey Mantle fan, led to Philip Jr. being called 'Mickey'. (Forget the story that his big protruding ears as a kid made him resemble Mickey Mouse.)

Rourke's mother, Anne, was to all intents and purposes a homemaker, although she trained and sometimes worked as a nurse. The Rourkes lived in a lower middle-class house in a lower middle-class neighbourhood. The family's maternal grandmother lived in their small basement apartment, where Mickey would seek safe haven during the frequent violent arguments between his parents.

When he was seven years old, Mickey, his half brother Joey and their little sister Patti were told by their mother that they and their grandmother were going to take a family trip to Miami. They were told that their father would follow them at a later date. Young Mickey could sense something was wrong, as most children perceptively can, and was resistant to the idea. The trip was being sold to him as a vacation, with the further enticement that the children were promised a pony.

Before the separation could be affected, Philip Sr. pulled young Mickey aside and explained the truth – their mother was breaking the family up. She was moving them away to a strange place where the children had never been before, and where they knew no one. Mickey was incensed, and refused outright to make the move. Soon the boy would become convinced of its inevitability. But his failure to deal with the reasons for his family's split would plant poisonous seeds in his psyche. It's one of the elements of his early life that haunt him to this day, that he constantly does battle with on a virtual daily basis. He would become indifferent, or outright hostile, toward authority figures, and would question his own sense of identity and self-worth.

Mickey did not hate his father. He admired him, and his dedication to fitness and athleticism. But he was also deeply resentful of what he was told of his father's significant role in the destruction of the family unit. From the moment that the Rourkes, *sans* Philip Sr., drove off towards Miami in search of a new life, Mickey lost all contact with him. He would not see his father for another two decades. But he would always carry Philip Sr.'s photo around with him, and would periodically formulate plans to reconnect with his father. These plans always went unfulfilled, leaving him feeling even more disillusioned, disappointed and empty.

Their arrival in Miami was uneventful, that first year feeling tentative. They lived in a few cheap motels. Mickey, Joey and Patti would pretty much keep to themselves, as they felt alien in this strange place, uncomfortable with their new surroundings and the negative circumstances that brought them there.

Anne would find comfort with the new man in her life, a Florida cop named Gene Addis. Almost exactly one year after they arrived in Miami, as soon as her divorce from Philip Sr. was finalised, she and Gene would marry. Being a career lawman, he was also a strict disciplinarian. Mickey felt immediately awkward around him, averse to his presence. Gene felt that his attitude toward the Rourke children was reasonable – after all, he suddenly had a very large family to provide for and maintain control over, bringing five boys of his own to the marriage. Gene was by most descriptions a decent man, a widower trying his damnedest to make his new marriage and new family work. He asked that the Rourke children refer to him as 'Dad', something Mickey flatly refused to do. He had no intention of allowing this man to usurp his father's place, and felt betrayed when his brother Joey took the path of least resistance.

The Rourke bunch would settle in a rough part of Miami called Liberty City, an area populated mostly by African-Americans and Cubans. They lived in a large apartment in the back of a coin laundromat that Anne owned and operated.

Young Mickey simply could not adjust to life with his new family. He had no use for his stepfather, and wasn't comfortable around the new stepbrothers he had to share a room with. The problematic feelings that began when he left Schenectady only deepened. He didn't want to be living in Liberty City, with these people, but as a kid he had no choice in the matter.

When Rourke speaks of his childhood, it is always with a kind of quiet poignancy. 'There is not much you can do at that age,' he has said. 'You either click on or you click off. And I clicked off for years. When you're a kid you wake up in the morning or you try to go to sleep at night and you say, "Why me? Why is this happening to me?" Now the way I look at it, honestly, all I can say is that I have two arms and two legs, a brother and a sister. I look at it that way now, but back then it was a nightmare.'

When Mickey was taken away from his real father against his will, he angrily told Philip Sr. that his behaviour would be just reward for the insensitivity shown to him. He vowed that he would never apply himself in school and would simply drift through life – refusing to care about it, as he clearly felt his father did not care about him. This was a vow Mickey would uncompromisingly keep. He sat at the back of the classroom and just passed time. His indifference was so complete that he was reassigned to a class for slow learners, and still showed nothing but slothful indifference. He only managed to keep himself afloat in school by cheating. 'I used to get my grandfather to do my homework for me, but he would do it all wrong,' he admits. 'His writing was also very messy so when I turned in my assignments to the teacher she knew that it wasn't me who did it.'

I asked Rourke about the root cause of the anger he said he carried with him throughout his adult life, growing ever more intense until those around him could also feel its effect. 'It wasn't until I started to get into therapy seriously that I realised that a lot of the stuff that was causing me problems was stuff that was still fucking me over from my childhood,' he explained.

Rourke's discomfort at home had a curious side effect. It would cause him to become an habitual liar. In an interview he gave early in his career, he said, 'If you grow up in harmony, let's call it, you don't have to lie. But if you live in disharmony, then you have to lie, and lie good. When I was a young kid I would start talking to friends, and I would start making shit up that would even amaze myself. I couldn't tell the truth if you hit me over the head with it. I'd be lying and really believing what I was saying. I noticed a lot of other guys doing it too. When you are so fucked up, confused and unhappy, you have to make shit up just to feel good. I think a certain amount of that probably helps me say other people's lines with conviction. That was the difference between me and my brother Joey. I would rather lie than get hit. My brother would never lie, no matter what.'

By the time Mickey reached his early teens, the family moved to Miami Beach. It was a much nicer neighbourhood than Liberty City, but again he had mixed feelings. He had grown used to living amongst the black kids, developing many friendships with kids who were every bit as disenfranchised as he felt himself to be. So when he and Joey hit Miami they were once again strangers in a strange land. They brought with them the attitude and the style that had been the norm in Liberty City, but which made them stand out like offensively lit neon signs: pointed shoes, white socks, oddly coloured t-shirts. 'They called us the Hooples – until one day my brother hit one of them over the head with a baseball bat. To them we were like the James gang. But we weren't really bad, we were just different.'

It was around his mid-teen years that Mickey threw himself headlong into sports. Both school and home life held nothing for him, but in sports he found that he could earn respect through his performance. He found also that he could develop feelings of self-worth that had long since lain dormant, and that he thrived on competitiveness. However, while his attraction to sports would effect a change in his outlook, he was not completely reformed just yet. His problems with authority figures were still intact, and were becoming more pronounced with each passing year.

One of the sports that Rourke excelled in was baseball. On his high school team he was considered one of the better players, but, because of a run-in with his coach over lack of commitment and missing practice, he was unceremoniously kicked off the team just days before a group of scouts came looking for future professional prospects.

A couple of seasons later, Mickey would volunteer as a coach for a Little League baseball team, and one of his players happened to be future Hollywood actor Andy Garcia. I later asked

Garcia what he remembered about Coach Rourke 'He was great, he was a really good coach,' came the response. 'He was very encouraging, but encouraging in his own way, not jumping up and down, but just making you feel good about your play with quiet comments about how great you were playing – he would always say things like, "hit it out of the park slugger, you've got it in you, out of the park, slugger."'

At this time Mickey also began his lifetime's involvement with boxing. He began training as a boxer at the age of fourteen at Miami's Fifth St. Gym, a place where another American fighter, by the name of Muhammad Ali, used to hang out and train. Rourke would train for four solid years as boxing became a major passion in his life. He had four bouts in the Police Athletic League, fighting out of the Northwest Boys Club, and won all four of them. This may seem like a minor achievement, but it was actually a much bigger deal. Most big-time American prizefighters began their careers by fighting in the Police Athletic League.

Mickey grew to love boxing, its physicality, the opportunity it provided to prove himself against another guy, one on one, no excuses, no time for second thoughts or indecision. But once again his lack of discipline, when it came to taking orders or instructions from authority figures, would keep him from advancing in the way that he desired. His trainers would tell him to do his roadwork (getting up at dawn and running for several miles) and Mickey would either make excuses or simply lie about having done it. (This situation would resurface again 25 years later, when he returned to boxing.)

His trainers at the time would press him to either make the commitment fully, or get the fuck out of boxing and stop wasting their time. They would tell him what he needed to do to improve and he would ignore them. They were losing their patience.

'I gave up boxing at the time because, although I was pretty good, I didn't understand the full extent of the commitment you have to make to become a real fighter, a professional fighter,' he admits.

But his early days in the ring would also leave a legacy that would come back to haunt him years later. Rourke suffered a couple of concussions during his time as an amateur fighter, and they were severe enough for the doctors who examined him to strongly advise he give up any plans of a future in the ring.

Rourke's friend of the time, Reid McBride, later remembered how he gravitated towards boxing in the first place because 'it was a direct way for him to release a lot of the anger that he had bottled up inside him'.

But Rourke's failure to follow through on his dream of becoming a professional boxer would also have a resonating psychological effect. One of the reasons he gives when asked about his ill-advised return to boxing at a fairly advanced age was how, back in the early days in Miami, he had left something unfulfilled that ate at him constantly.

Without boxing, Rourke's life in Miami was aimless. He and his brother and their pals frequented the area of town known as Little Havana. They would dress up like dandy dudes, sit in coffee shops and smoke huge Cuban cigars. Mickey was hooked on his platform shoes, tight pants and cut-off shirts. 'I don't know why I dressed like that,' he later said in an interview. 'I just liked those dudes that I was hanging with because they were loose, they weren't uptight. We had nothing on our minds but a good fucking time.' Rourke would go on to make the amusing disclosure, 'I don't think I ever talked to a nice girl until I was about 25 years old – all the girls that I was with during that time were the other kind.'

During this time of drifting and aimlessness, he would have his one and only brush with drug use. The way Rourke tells it, 'During the day we would go down to the 48th St. Beach. We would wear these tiny little bathing suits and lay in the sun all day, we would take half a dozen Seconals, and we were big on downers back then. Everyone would talk in slow motion, everybody would be checking each other out. And you never heard such bragging and lying. We were all into being cool, being tough, getting down and getting high.' He goes on to clarify his statement with a tinge of sadness. 'I am totally fucking anti drugs. I had my fling with them, but it wasn't for long. All those guys back then, a lot of them aren't around anymore, a lot of them are dead.'

As he was knocking around Miami Beach, looking for odd jobs to make a bit of money whenever the urge struck him, he would try a multitude of different things. He was a machinist for one single day – although he was shown how to operate a machine that bent pipes, he wasn't paying attention and ended up just sitting and staring at the machine all day. He was an usher in a movie theatre for a spell, but got into a fight with another usher and was fired after the other guy 'conked me over the head with a flashlight.'

Rourke loved the movies, but not because he had any aspirations to be an actor. It was because of screen icons like Marlon Brando, Steve McQueen and Lee Marvin. This was not the geekazoid hero worship of guys like Quentin Tarantino and Brett Ratner. It was a more subtle kind of yearning that whispered in Mickey's head that, if he watched these guys enough times, he might become like them in some way. Rourke's friend and fellow movie fan Reid McBride remembered, 'Yeah, the guy we liked to watch the most was Marlon Brando – McQueen too, but Brando was the guy who really inspired us in a way that a cool, rebellious icon can . . . like what Mickey actually became himself.' Brando and McQueen both grew up with identity issues, with distant or strained relationships to their fathers.

Rourke's drifting would lead him into such dead-end occupations as laying linoleum, working construction, working in a warehouse, and then, fatefully, a job working as a pool boy at a local hotel that provided a decisive turning point. One of the guys that he worked with, cleaning the pool and laying out the lounge chairs, did some theatrical acting while attending a local community college. When the group were staging Jean Genet's *Death Watch*, this friend thought that his old pool pal Mickey might like a little of this action himself. (Theatre always attracted the best looking, most free spirited women.)

He called Mickey and suggested he take on the role of 'Green Eyes'. Rourke had no idea why this guy thought he might make an actor, and was further bewildered by his own decision to attend. 'I went down there and did this Genet thing with him. It was about this black guy and this white guy on death row. I really liked it, I don't think I was very good at it, you know, in this first thing, but I really liked it. It was a great feeling, I didn't particularly know what it was, but it felt good.' Rourke reprised his performance at a few other colleges around the state, and would later describe the experience as 'the first worthwhile thing that I had done in four years.'

Rourke had moved out on his own by this time, and was living with five other guys in a

**13**

small hotel in Miami Beach called the Wild West. The novelty of living just to 'get radical' was starting to wear thin. Then one day, while stretched out on the beach with a friend from the area, a character they called Stoney Curtis – because of his propensity for getting high, combined with his resemblance to Tony Curtis – a revelation came to Mickey Rourke. Stoney had just gotten out of jail after serving time for some minor robbery beef, and was back on the beach trying to enlist Mickey's help in his latest larcenous scheme. Suddenly Rourke piped up and said, 'No man, I'm going to be an actor. I'm going to New York.' This wasn't something that he had been seriously planning, or even given much thought to. But he asked someone during the run of the Genet play where he could go to learn more about acting, to train seriously. He was told that New York was where Brando, McQueen, Jimmy Dean and Montgomery Clift had all started.

So Rourke left the beach and Stoney Curtis behind. He borrowed $400 from his sister Patti and boarded a plane for the short hop to New York City. It was worlds away from the life he had known, but he was directing his own show now, making a decision to do something positive and life affirming.

# Chapter Two

# NEW YORK ON A DIME

## 'I like New York. I feel alive in New York, a lot more alive than I feel in that other place.' – *Mickey Rourke*

Going to New York City for the first time is always an experience to be reckoned with, no matter who you are or how cool you believe yourself to be. It will humble you with its size, its scope, its hustle and bustle, and the legend that always precedes it. But the funny thing is that, once you return after that first visit, you feel differently, more comfortable and at ease with everything about that grand city.

When Mickey Rourke hit the streets of New York in 1975, he was nineteen years old. Hearing him talk about the experience today, you would think it was part of a comedy sketch, but for a green-as-grass kid it was a daunting experience. Rourke was coming to New York City from Miami, the polar opposite in terms of climate, appearance and attitude. Miami's laid-back attitude originates from its sunshine, bright colours, heat and music. New York City is a gargantuan organism that lives and breathes on its own, and makes allowances for no one. If you enter into its energy, you had better keep moving onward and upward, or, as Dickens said, 'You will be ploughed under with the weak and the infirmed.'

Mickey Rourke's Miami swagger carried zero weight in New York City. He was so filled with misconceptions about the place that it's a miracle he survived his first night there. His know-it-all Miami pals told Rourke that you must never take a cab in New York City driven by a black driver. If you hail a cab and the driver is black – just wave him on. So when Rourke arrived in town he stood outside LaGuardia Airport and waved on cab after cab, until finally he found one driven by a Russian and climbed in.

He told the driver to take him directly to the Actor's Studio. Arriving at the studio, a structure that is less than impressive from the outside, he walked in with his suitcase in hand. Luckily, he found a sympathetic instructor who allowed him to come in and relax and watch some of the classes that were being conducted. After several hours the instructor suggested that it might be a good time for him to head home. When Rourke explained that when he said he had just arrived in town, he had meant it literally, the instructor wished him well but explained that he could not allow him to stay there. Rourke didn't actually think that he could bunk at the Actor's Studio, but his trip to New York was made so impetuously that he never actually made any plans.

With help from another cab driver, Rourke found his first home in New York City – a $35 a week hotel. Rourke's suite was small and dingy and dirty. He slept at night with a baseball bat (a going away present from his paranoid pals in Miami) beside him in bed and a chair propped against the already locked door. Mickey had virtually no prospects of work lined up, and was very limited in terms of funds. He was living in a place filled with people in similar circumstances or worse, and because he was still in Miami mode (pastel colours, platform shoes) he was put upon by every gay chicken hawk that crossed his path. He realised very quickly that he should have come up with something resembling a plan.

I asked Rourke about those early days in New York, 30 years after the fact. 'It was rough for a while,' he said. 'I was there with a purpose in mind, and I knew what I wanted to do, I had no fucking clue about how to go about doing it. There were times when I was broke, broker than broke. But I always found a way to keep it going.'

Rourke had help in keeping it going from his benevolent grandmother. She would send him monthly stipends that, while they were deeply appreciated, still only kept him perpetually a little bit behind. Even with her help there were days on end when Rourke was so broke that he survived on potato chips and chocolate bars – all the while keeping his eye on the calendar for the next trip to Western Union, to collect his grandmother's blessing.

And like the classic struggling actor that he was, Mickey then drifted from one dead-end job to another – everything from working in a whorehouse as an attendant/bouncer to moving furniture in a warehouse. (The same furniture warehouse had employed such former struggling actors as Gene Hackman, Steve McQueen and Lee Marvin.)

Once Rourke had managed to get himself together in New York, he moved from the dive he was living in to a relatively better class of dive – a hotel on West Eighth Street called the Marlton. It was during his stay at this place that things would begin to take shape. Not that Rourke could see it at the time, but things were starting to shift in his favour. 'It was a weird place, the Marlton, I was in the "penthouse" but that really just meant I was on the top floor, the room was no bigger or any more luxurious,' said Rourke. 'The place was filled with pimps and hustlers and transvestites and the bathroom was so full of holes used by perverts to spy on people in the bathroom that I had to spend a half hour before taking a bath plugging all the fucking holes with wet toilet paper.'

At the time, Mickey was living with a friend of his from Miami, a guy called Little Eddie, who was not above doing just about anything at all for money. Because Rourke is loyal almost to a fault, he nearly allowed himself to get sucked into some of Little Eddie's schemes – ranging from minor-league drug dealing to two-bit burglary and selling stolen goods. But at the same time, he was also being nudged in a much more positive direction by one of the managers of the Marlton, a guy named Carl Montgomery.

Montgomery was the hotel's night manager, but he was also a major fan of the theatre. He had a large collection of Broadway playbills that Rourke would spend hours pouring over, having been influenced by the infectious enthusiasm of his friend. Rourke looked at the actors and read about the plays. He found himself growing more and more excited about the theatre, and felt a conviction that acting would give someone a way of creating a whole new world for himself, of exploring different facets of life and experience. A world that a guy could completely lose himself in.

Montgomery took Mickey to his first Broadway play, deepening his fascination for the process. For Montgomery was not just a friend but also something of a guru. He helped Rourke change his style from that of a Miami pimp to a more New York kind of look and attitude, which is a style Mickey maintains to this very day.

Rourke would return to the Actor's Studio every once in a while, to try to gain entry into the venerable school of the Method, but it was tough. Criteria for gaining entry was entirely up to the discretion of the main man, the legendary Lee Strasberg.

A lot of actors swore by the teachings of Strasberg and the Method. The Method is simply a style or discipline of acting that dictates that the actor uses his own life experiences, his own inner voice and emotions, to infuse whatever character he is playing with a kind of inherent truth. But some others – like Marlon Brando in particular – thought Strasberg's championing of the Method was about nothing more than the gigantic ego of a failed actor.

Rourke would have mixed feelings about the studio. He badly wanted to get into the school because actors talked about it as *the* place to train. But once he gained admittance, he began to feel differently. 'I got a lot of good stuff out of the place, I got connected to the best acting teacher in the world there,' said Rourke. 'But what was weird was that in the classes there was like Al Pacino and Chris Walken who were actually doing some work, and everyone else in the class had never done a fucking thing, that always struck me as weird that out of the whole place there were just two guys doing professional stuff.'

At the time, Christopher Walken was a brilliant talent on the New York stage, doing everything from Shakespeare to Brecht, but had only had a few small roles on film (like *Annie Hall* and the Sidney Lumet thriller *The Anderson Tapes*). Al Pacino, on the other hand, had already established himself as a soaring new screen presence. One of the need breed of Method anti-heroes, he had dazzled audiences with his work in *Panic in Needle Park*, *The Godfather Parts I and II*, *Serpico*, and his near flawless performance in *Dog Day Afternoon*. Pacino and Walken would return to the Actor's Studio in much the same way that professional bodybuilders return to the gym to workout, even after they have won championships.

At the Actor's Studio, actors with different levels of professional experience or training worked with different teachers. After Rourke finally gained admittance, he fell under the guidance of a teacher named Sandra Seacat. An attractive woman who projected a strength and power that belied her soft voice (something that has also been said of Mickey Rourke), Seacat was a staunch believer in the teachings of the originator of the Method, the Russian actor Konstantin Stanislavski.

Seacat saw something in Rourke that she believed was special. As she'd later say, 'Mickey's instincts were very natural, like an animal's instincts.' But it took some time for Rourke to connect with her on a level where he was comfortable enough to open up. With his troubled past, he found it very hard to reveal anything private or personal about his feelings. Even while he was attending classes regularly, he didn't always actively participate. He had spent years building up a defence mechanism as a survival technique, a wall around his emotional self – lowering that wall was not something he could easily do. As Rourke described it, 'Acting wasn't a normal sort of thing to do, I used to see people in class and I didn't know what the fuck they were doing. I know what they were getting at now, but then I had no fucking clue, it took me a couple of years to get to that place.'

Sandra Seacat did not give up on Rourke. 'She saw something in me worth her time and attention,' he said. 'It was the first real guidance I ever had, I probably would not have stuck with acting had it not been for her. She made everything click.'

His turning point as an acting student came one day when Rourke was frustrated by how other students were getting up and doing improvisations, with no apparent difficulty. Seacat then told Rourke to get up in front of the class and perform solo, acting as if he was shining shoes. He did as he was instructed, and almost immediately got lost in the physicality of the action. Before he knew it he was breaking down in tears, as the focus on simple physical movements conjured up gentle memories of childhood that still lived within him. He recalled the sunny summer days at the baseball diamond with his dad; the memory of his father kneeling before him and tying his shoes for him gently and carefully, making sure they were tied tightly but comfortably. He found himself pouring out emotions that had been pent up for years.

It was the moment when Mickey Rourke knew that, not only could he be an actor, he already *was* an actor. 'I'm a very slow learner,' he later said. 'I was a late bloomer when it came to growing up. It took me quite a few years to get my stuff together because I had no great drive to be an actor. There is a large part of me that doesn't want to open up. As an actor you have to open up, I spent my whole life keeping things to myself and all of a sudden I am going to completely let it out?'

Once the breakthrough came, Rourke's lifelong attitude of no-compromise almost stopped his progress as an actor dead in its tracks. With Sandra Seacat's help, he began getting work in some off-Broadway productions. But he would never do anything that seemed to him to be phony or artificial, so a lot of the time he would be cast in shows, then argue with the director, and end up leaving before he even got to perform before an audience.

I asked Rourke about his first acting jobs: 'It was a strange time, a strange thing, I knew I wanted to do this, but I really wasn't sure why, so I just went with what my gut was telling me.'

Seacat wanted more from him, and pushed Rourke to try to deal with some of the elements of his personal life that would allow him to connect with his acting roles in a deeper, more profound way. Seacat convinced him that, before he auditioned for an Actor's Studio production of *Cat on a Hot Tin Roof*, he should make the effort to reconnect with his own father. Rourke trusted Seacat, who so far seemed to have nothing but his best interests at heart. He boarded a bus for Schenectady, where he finally got to spend time with his father for the first time in over fifteen years.

It was not one of those Hollywood family reunion scenes. Rourke remembers it as a strange meeting. 'Yeah, I was really in a weird place. I was there and was conscious of being there, but in my head I was actually playing the character [Brick] the whole time, so I never really connected with the event.' Rourke was always impressed with the good shape that his father had kept himself in. So when he saw that Philip Sr. had let himself go, and that the muscles he was so proud of developing had gone soft and flabby, it caused more disillusionment. Rourke's only emotional protection was that he was already playing in character.

He left Schenectady with $50 that his father had offered him and headed back to the city, convinced that he now had the elements he needed to pull off the performance. It was the last time he would ever see his father.

*The young Rourke in his second notable screen role, as charming womaniser and gambler Boogie in Barry Levinson's* Diner *(1982).*

One of the personal high points of Mickey Rourke's time at the Actor's Studio was his developing friendship with Christopher Walken, whom he admired both as an actor and as a man. Rourke and Walken would go on to work together several times: in the film *Heaven's Gate*, that Walken pitched Rourke for; in *Homeboy*, a low-budget film developed by Rourke; *Man on Fire* and *Domino*. Rourke liked Walken as an actor, because he was not an obvious leading man in terms of his looks, and didn't take himself (as opposed to his work) too seriously.

One of his Actor's Studio roles that Rourke found the most stimulating came in their production of Shakespeare's *Richard III*. His role was a small one, playing Richard's page, but, while the Shakespearean language had little in common with his own way of speaking, he instinctively connected with it.

But while this was a time of great personal discovery, confusing notions about what it was to be an actor also started to creep in. The overwhelming odds against anyone making a living as an actor, no matter how talented, were confusing and daunting. 'I saw guys at the Actor's Studio who were a lot older than I was, who had been attending classes and doing productions there for years,' said Rourke. 'But these guys had done fuck all professionally as actors. Then I go to the movies and see kids with no particular talent making a quarter of a million bucks for a movie. I just couldn't understand it.'

The dilemma also caused him to take a second look at the whole Actor's Studio experience. 'You work and you do classes and do workshops and do productions in the Actor's Studio and you feel like an artist,' said Rourke. 'But you know what, who cares? Like who the fuck really cares, what does it all amount to? I am glad that I went there and did the stuff that I did there but it was then that I decided that I had to stick to my own set of rules.'

Rourke was also not terribly fond of criticism. As far as he could see, it was only heaped upon him when the Actor's Studio wanted to flex some authoritarian muscles. Sandra Seacat remembers, 'Mickey was a purist, it was all or nothing for him, so when he felt like he wasn't being treated the way he needed to be treated, he clashed with Strasberg.'

One day, during a workshop with Lee Strasberg, the master himself, Rourke found himself on the receiving end of a really heavy licking. He disconnected instantly from the Actor's Studio and walked out, never to return again.

But Rourke's confidence continued to grow under Seacat's guidance, when he was cast in the role of Eddie, the main character in Arthur Miller's play *A View from the Bridge*. While this performance was staged more as a special workshop presentation by Seacat, it was viewed by Miller himself, who had nothing but praise for Rourke's interpretation. It was this performance that brought forth the first suggestion that Rourke should maybe consider heading West, and taking a stab at Hollywood. Seacat knew that he had something out of the ordinary, and encouraged him to do it.

But Rourke had finally started to feel comfortable in New York, to really enjoy the glow that came from becoming the thing that he had feared – a big star, but only in acting classes. Seacat could see it coming. While she had indulged him for a while, she finally lowered the boom. When asked about that moment, Rourke pinned it down to specific details: 'It was pouring rain and we were standing on the corner of Eighth Avenue – she was yelling at me and shoving me and really fucking laying into me – asking me if I wanted to be a professional class taker or if I wanted to be an actor – she kept yelling, "Do something, get out there and work!"'

Using some of the connections he had made, Rourke secured a manager in Hollywood – a guy named Bob LeMond, who, with his partner Louis Zetter, would be credited with shepherding the early career of John Travolta along. There were no promises made, but LeMond said that if Rourke could make it out West, they would see what they could do about securing him an agent and trying to get him connected.

Rourke once again borrowed enough money to get out to California, but was so short of cash when he arrived in Los Angeles that he needed to find a job right away. After a day of walking up and down the only street in Los Angeles he knew by name, Sunset Boulevard, he finally found a job as a valet for a restaurant.

LeMond and Zetter were good to their word. They got Rourke meetings and interviews, but the agents seemed largely indifferent to him – either telling him, 'go back to New York, where your kind of acting is done,' or else saying that he had promise and that they'd love to represent him, only to never get back to him. Then he was introduced to a younger guy named Bernie Carneol, who ran his own agency and was of the same headstrong attitude as Rourke.

When Rourke and Carneol met, the agent was instantly intrigued. He thought that Rourke had a freshness, a uniqueness about him that he could sell to producers and directors. He told Rourke to go away and prepare two monologues, one a contemporary piece and the other taken from a classic play or novel. Rourke did as he was instructed – he came back to Carneol's office a few days later and performed them for his potential new agent.

After watching him, Carneol slid an agreement across his desk towards Rourke for his signature.

The job of the Hollywood agent is to get his clients meetings, to get their names and pictures out there, to field offers – but most of all, their job is to get their clients work, any kind of acting work at all. Carneol proved himself up to the job, instantly getting Rourke small roles and day work on a number of TV serials and movies of the week. 'He worked his ass off for me,' said Rourke. 'So naturally I wanted to live up to whatever confidence he was showing in me.'

Carneol was trying to get Rourke enough work so that a 'reel' could be assembled as quickly as possible. A reel is a series of brief clips gathered onto one tape that illustrates what the client has done for producers as a way of creating interest.

Mickey Rourke's early Hollywood experience was eye opening – a lot of the things he was doing he felt to be pointless, until he was taught that there was no such thing as a bad opportunity in Hollywood, only wasted opportunities. With every role you are hired to play, you are presented with a chance to increase your visibility.

He was about to make a breakthrough against all the odds. But at first glance, even this breakthrough wasn't all it was cracked up to be.

# Chapter Three

**'For the people all said, "Beware, you're on a heavenly trip." And the people all said, "Beware, because you'll scuttle the ship – And the devil will drag you under."'**
**– Nicely Nicely Johnson, Guys and Dolls**

'Working on that film almost made me want to give up on film acting altogether,' said Mickey Rourke when I asked him about his first ever big screen role.

Those unique qualities that people had been speaking of started to gain the attention of producers and directors, just as his agent said they would. The TV work led to a couple of shots at the big screen – the earliest being a blink-and-you'll-miss-it part in the big-budget flop *1941*. The film is not really as bad as a lot of people will have you believe, despite the fact that it's often listed in books and magazine articles as one of the biggest bombs in movie history. Its comedic story fictionalised a tiny incident from WWII, when a single Japanese submarine drifted too close to the shores of Southern California in the days after the bombing of Pearl Harbor, setting off a wave of mass hysteria entirely out of proportion to the threat that existed.

In 1978, when the script was given the green light, it had already been kicking around awhile. John Milius (co-writer of *Apocalypse Now*/writer-director of *Conan the Barbarian*) had worked with a couple of young writers named Bob Gale and Robert Zemeckis, the future A-list director, on some ideas that Gale thought would make a great black comedy in the vein of *Dr. Strangelove*. Two different Hollywood studios agreed to finance the potentially very expensive film, once *wunderkind* director Steven Spielberg agreed to make it. The steam it built up made it seem like as sure a bet as was ever wagered in Hollywood. Spielberg was coming off two massive hits in a row – his 1975 film *Jaws* was not only a massive critical and commercial success but set new commercial expectations. If a film could not break the $100 million mark, it simply was not considered a hit anymore. He followed that with the eye-popping science fiction *tour de force, Close Encounters of the Third Kind*. For his next project, both Universal Pictures (the studio that produced *Jaws*) and Columbia Pictures (the studio responsible for *Close Encounters*) agreed to take on the financing and distribution in tandem.

Spielberg saw *1941* as his chance to make a big, splashy Hollywood musical comedy. But the film began to go haywire almost as soon as it began. The stars were comic actors John Belushi (whose legendary drug use – detailed in Bob Woodward's book *Wired* – would kill him at the young age of 32) and his TV comedy partner Dan Aykroyd. Many of the reports from the set, including those by the cast of Canadian comedy show *SC-TV*, described the experience as a great big Hollywood frat party. There were also darker claims that drug use was so rampant on the set that there were provisions built into the budget for the purchase of cocaine.

The movie is a loud, silly mess, but still somewhat enjoyable. But a lot of it is just one big Hollywood in-joke that audiences simply did not share in. It opens with a scene of actor Susan Backaline stripping nude and going for a late night skinny dip as the Japanese submarine is surfacing – Backaline is the girl who strips nude and goes for a fatal late night skinny-dip in *Jaws*. Later, when the character of Wild Bill Kelso (Belushi) is introduced, the visual presentation of the scene is exactly like the opening sequence of *Close Encounters.*

Mickey Rourke took a small role in the film, as Private Reese, on the advice of his agent that he should jump at the opportunity to be in a film directed by Spielberg – something that is even truer now than it was then. Rourke can only be glimpsed briefly in a few scenes, mostly in the background. But, as scanty as his performance is, he was featured prominently in one of the lobby card stills used for the film's release in France.

When I asked Rourke about the film, he smiled uncomfortably and shook his head. When he told me that he had almost quit acting after the experience, I wasn't sure if he was serious or just being flippant. I asked him to elaborate. 'I just saw what was going on around me,' said Rourke. 'That film, a big Hollywood production, it kind of freaked me out a bit that the acting part of the scene seemed to be the last thing on the priority list after the stunts and the technical stuff. It really didn't feel like acting to me.'

I asked Rourke for his opinion on Spielberg and his movies in general. 'Hey man, the guy does what he does better than anyone else does, probably better than anyone else has ever done,' he said. 'But you have to dig that sort of thing. It is like some silly pop group that gets really successful, there is no denying that they are selling millions of records and are very popular – that don't mean that everyone has to listen to it or to like it.'

Rourke was a mass of conflicting emotions after this experience. He now believed he might actually be able to pull off a career as a professional actor, but he was relatively new to the process and his footing unsure.

He would also appear in a far less ambitious big screen offering called *Fade to Black*, a horror movie. But it was the hard work of his agent that ensured things started to advance in the way he had hoped. Rourke now found himself reading for larger parts in TV movies, projects he rarely talks about now, even though his work in them is nothing at all to be ashamed of. He played the first of three hefty TV roles in a very interesting, well thought-out drama called *City in Fear*, starring veteran actor David Janssen (who did not live to see the film aired).

*City in Fear* was three hours long, and asked an interesting question about the role of the media in our society: Is it manipulating us, or is the media itself being manipulated by government and law enforcement agencies to suit their own purposes? The story revolves around a burned-out journalist who is convinced by a cynical, sensationalist editor to follow and report on the activities of a serial killer. But the killer, played by Rourke, starts to like the notoriety and commits crimes just because the media coverage excites him. Janssen plays the journalist, and delivers one of the finer performances of his career, while Robert Vaughn is the editor. Rourke is not in the film nearly as much as the aforementioned two, but he makes an impact. He hams it up a bit as the homicidal maniac, but has the natural acting ability to make these affectations interesting rather than just obvious. Rourke had a set of instinctual chops, or techniques, certain hand gestures or facial expressions, that he would use from this early performance right on up through his heavily made-up role as Marv in *Sin City*.

There must have been some creative problems on the film, because the director, Jud Taylor, took his name off of it and assigned it to that tried and tested pseudonym, Alan Smithee. But writer Alan Ruben won the 1981 Edgar Allan Poe Award for Excellence in Television Writing for his *City in Fear* teleplay, and the film stays taut and suspenseful throughout its extended running time.

Jud Taylor also directed another TV movie with Rourke, who was third billed in *Act of Love*. Again, it told a very sensitive story in a non-sensational way. An adventurous young man is paralysed after a motorcycle accident; his young brother, played by Ron Howard, helps him take his own life in a so-called mercy killing. It's a standard movie of the week, with a few tugs at the heartstrings, offering up a controversial theme which it then sugarcoats to make as palatable as possible. Rourke is okay, but is hampered by a weak script that leaves out the hardest hitting aspects of the story. At times he seems to be just walking through the film, doing no more than what is expected of him.

Rourke's third TV movie would offer him the best opportunity to show his raw talents. Another factually based story, *Rape and Marriage: The Rideout Case* dealt with the strange case of an Oregon woman, Greta Rideout, who set a rather courageous precedent when she had her abusive husband arrested for rape. The court case that followed made headlines around the world and was the cause of considerable discussion and debate. Rourke played John Rideout, the husband and accused rapist, and was simply terrific. There were moments in his performance where he was touching on histrionics, but it showed the depth of his abilities in terms of both natural instinct and acquired technique. During the most intense moments in the film, Rourke lashes out with shocking ferocity at whatever is at hand, whether it be a door or his wife – that sudden unleashed fury would become part of almost every subsequent performance he would give on film.

The character of Rideout is as unsympathetic as can be imagined, but Rourke, to his credit, brought a dimension of humanity to what could have been nothing more than a drooling redneck rapist portrayal. It's one of his best early performances, loaded with affectation but controlled and resonant.

Linda Hamilton (*The Terminator, T2: Judgment Day*) played Greta with equal effectiveness, quiet and humble, but with a streak of courage that allows her to take action against all advice and her own better judgement. Her scenes with Rourke crackle with tension and emotion.

Rourke himself was noticeably maturing as an actor. He had now handled roles of different sizes and dimensions for directors who ranged from superstars to journeymen, and was arriving at that place where what is expected of you and what you want to do start to come together.

It was at this point that he found himself at a fork in the road. Professionally, he was getting work and he was getting noticed. But he was also living on the profligate side, and would go through his money about as fast as he was earning it. Rourke and Carneol had their sights set on landing something substantial in a feature film, but the actor was worried about holding out for one of those special roles that rarely ever arrive.

He had gone through the money he had earned thus far, and found himself working as a bouncer at a transvestite club in a seedy section of Hollywood Boulevard. He was offered a role in a soap opera-ish mini series, but, even though the payday was in the neighbourhood of half a million bucks, turned it down flat without even reading the script. As a testament to how seriously Carneol was taking Rourke's development, it was *he* who advised his client not to touch the script, but to hang on a little longer until he found something that would make a difference. Carneol explained to Rourke that he had been getting very positive feedback from producers and directors, with greater and greater frequency. Rourke dug in and kept faith.

Things were also happening in Rourke's personal life as well. Not long after arriving in Los Angeles, he'd met a pretty, headstrong young actress named Debra Feuer when they were both working bit parts in a TV crime drama called *Hard Case*. They quickly formed a bond.

'I didn't really know what to make of him at first,' said Feuer. 'He was in character almost all the time, in this case the small role he was playing was of a guy who was very rough around the edges, constantly dirty, and who spoke with a Southern drawl. He struck me initially as a very strange guy.'

What was initially a bond between actors working closely together on a film, something that happens with great frequency on movie sets, grew into something deeper. Feuer was attracted to his eccentricity, and also to the sensitive side of his personality that he tended to keep buried. 'He would show up at my door even though I had a boyfriend,' she said. 'But my boyfriend and I were almost done so I allowed myself to explore this thing that was happening with Mickey.'

Debra Feuer is of Belgian extraction. Her brother Ian was a well-known soccer player, who played in England for West Ham United and in Belgium for RWD Molenbeek. When she came to Los Angeles to pursue a life in the movies, she found a fair amount of work on episodes of *The Love Boat* and similarly superficial shows. Feuer had a bubbly personality, she smiled and laughed easily. But there was also a hint of toughness behind that bright smile, something that would cause casting directors to take a second look at her.

This was the first real relationship that Rourke had had with someone close to his own age, that extended beyond the fun of the first couple of nights. Before Debra, he had shown a definite preference for older women. Rourke describes his relationship with Debra Feuer as the first 'real' relationship he ever had, his previous dalliances being almost purely recreational in nature.

As their relationship bloomed, Rourke asked Debra out on a date to discuss something he described as being very important to him – and, he hoped, to her as well. He showed up at her home, nattily dressed with his hair slicked back, behind the wheel of a Cadillac convertible. When they went out for a drive and something to eat, Feuer noticed that Rourke was nervous, not saying much at all. Finally, after about an half an hour, he began to speak the words that had been wedged tightly in his throat. He asked her to marry him. Instinctively, Debra said yes to his proposal. Not longer after, they were married on a cliff-side in the bright sunshine of Palos Verdes, California. Mickey Rourke and Debra Feuer married almost a year to the day after they first met.

But before his wedding, Rourke would connect with the role that he was waiting for. And things would never be the same again.

# Chapter Four

# MICKEY AND MICHAEL

## 'Creativity is a drug that I cannot live without.' – *Cecil B. DeMille*

John Wayne and John Ford had it. Humphrey Bogart and John Huston had it. Robert De Niro and Martin Scorsese share it, as do John Woo and Chow Yun-Fat – that special symbiotic relationship that forms ever so rarely between actor and director. Woo told me that Chow was almost like an alter ego to him, the man that Woo wished he could be – suave, handsome, tall, fearless. And because of that they developed a kind of shorthand when it came to working together. The same can be said of the collaborations between Mickey Rourke and the mercurial filmmaker Michael Cimino.

To understand their films together, it is first necessary to get a glimpse of just who Michael Cimino is, and the impact he had on Hollywood during the last great epoch of American cinema. He was, for a time in the late Seventies, one of the hottest writer-directors around. Cimino could easily have become one of the greatest American filmmakers of all time, had he not fallen victim to a potent mix of timing, his own ego, and the turning tide of American moviemaking.

Cimino was born in New York City on 3 February, 1939. The date is questionable, however, as Cimino has always officially declared himself to be younger (and taller) than he actually is. (Since Cimino stands a full five feet five inches tall, and is rabidly self-conscious about it, he often wears cowboy boots with a substantial heel to compensate.) In his early days, Cimino simultaneously studied dramatic arts and architecture. But with his intentions set on becoming a filmmaker, he drifted into the world of PR and advertising, becoming a prolific director of television commercials. When he started making serious overtures to the studios, the neophyte filmmaker arrived at meetings driving the Rolls Royce he bought from the earnings.

In 1972, Cimino got his first screen credit for co-writing the screenplay (with Derek Washburn) for the directorial debut of special effects wizard Douglas Trumball, a compelling science fiction film called *Silent Running*.

His stock in Hollywood took another jump when Clint Eastwood hired him to work on the much anticipated sequel to his hit *Dirty Harry*, called *Magnum Force*. His co-writer on that project was John Milius, who would be instrumental in Mickey Rourke's first film, *1941*, and would contribute the first couple of drafts of *Apocalypse Now* – which ultimately went head to head with

Cimino's *The Deer Hunter*, to be the first big, controversial Vietnam film to make it into theatres. (Cimino's film won the competition.)

*Magnum Force* turned out to be a hit too, and Cimino found a powerful friend in Eastwood. He liked the way Cimino wrote, and the fact that the material was delivered efficiently and promptly. Cimino had mentioned from the start that directing a feature film was his ultimate ambition. Eastwood had been known to reward collaborators with their first projects as director, and the opportunity to make a film for his company, Malpaso Productions, came less than a year later, with a heist film called *Thunderbolt and Lightfoot*.

Eastwood is also known as a tough taskmaster, which is why his films often come in under budget and ahead of schedule. He told the young Michael Cimino that, if he was to allow him this opportunity, there would be 50 days to shoot the film and $7.5 million to make it. The new director shouldn't ask for one cent or one day more, or he would be replaced instantly, most likely by Eastwood himself.

*Thunderbolt and Lightfoot* turned out to be a great little film about people on the fringes of society, the criminal element who have feelings and dreams and wishes just like everyone else. Cimino made fantastic use of the Western USA's dramatic landscape, and got a performance out of 23-year-old Jeff Bridges that earned him an Oscar nomination for Best Supporting Actor, for his role as a brash young drifter who idolises Eastwood's legendary thief, 'the Thunderbolt'. Cimino wrote a terrific script and did a solid, professional job, bringing the film in on time and slightly under budget. It was released to critical acclaim and decent box-office returns, and the confidence Eastwood had shown in the new director inspired the studios to take a chance on him too.

It would take a couple of years of development for Cimino's magnum opus to be realised, as its subject matter was considered uncomfortable at the time. He was attempting to mount a grand epic about the Vietnam War and the effect it had on Americans. This was at a time when the wounds of that war were still very fresh and open, and showed no signs of closing. When Cimino began to discuss his plans for the film, called *The Deer Hunter*, the war had only been officially over for two years. So while every studio wanted to work with a talent like Cimino's, none were interested in risking millions on a film they felt sure no audience would want to see. But with a stubborn persistence, Cimino got his film made through a series of financial arrangements with a largely British group of producers – and what he delivered was damn near a masterpiece.

*The Deer Hunter* would become an event film. Initially released in a very limited number of theatres, word of mouth generated such interest that it would set house records virtually everywhere it played. The subsequent wider release made it a smash hit financially as well as critically. But the film was not without controversy, most of it stemming from the over-exuberance of Cimino himself. Seemingly drunk on the success of the film, he started giving interview after interview that seemed to grow in their levels of self-aggrandisement. He would allude to personal service in the Green Berets during the Vietnam War, something that was simply not true. Then some of the specific events of the film were called into question, even though Cimino insisted it was well researched and authentic. A major set piece in the film involved American POWs in North Vietnam being forced to engage in games of Russian Roulette by their captors. While the scenes were well shot, and acted with a riveting intensity, there was not a shred of evidence that anything remotely like it ever happened. (Cimino would be forced to clarify this incident as a 'metaphor' for America's adventuring in Vietnam.)

*The Deer Hunter* would go on to win well-deserved Oscars for Best Picture and Best Director, and for Christopher Walken as Best Supporting Actor. It is an epic in every sense of the word, with moments of breathtaking grandeur and depth. It also contains the first hints of Cimino's gargantuan tendency towards self-indulgence, that would completely consume him shortly thereafter.

The success of *The Deer Hunter* put Cimino into a whole new stratosphere, and it was up there, in that thin air, that his ego would expand to unreasonable proportions.

For his next epic, Cimino claimed humble beginnings. On a cross country flight, he read a magazine article about the invention of barbed wire, which then led into a deeper exploration of what became known as the Johnson County War: when rich landowners attempted to thwart early waves of immigrants from Eastern Europe by killing them all. Cimino would tell this story as a grand, revisionist Western about the real birth of modern America, about the rich building their wealth on the backs of the poor. But he would make the film like the classic Westerns he grew up on.

The story of the making of *Heaven's Gate*, the cost overages and the in-fighting, has been the subject of numerous magazine and newspaper articles. (There is an excellent book by ex-United Artists executive Steven Bach called *Final Cut*, and a feature-length documentary based on the book and narrated by Jeff Bridges, who co-starred in the film.) Budgeted originally at $12 million, the film was underwritten by United Artists, who had backed previous toughies like *Raging Bull* and *Apocalypse Now*. They saw their initial commitment inflate to an estimated $36 million in 1979 dollars. (Today, $36 million is considered a standard budget.) It brought United Artists to their knees, and then ultimately forced them to go under completely.

By the time the film previewed as an event presentation, it was deemed to be an ego-driven, self-indulgent, unqualified disaster. I remember waiting in line to pay an increased admission price for a roadshow-like early preview of *Heaven's Gate*, at the old University Theatre in Toronto. Cimino was in attendance, with girlfriend and producer Joann Carelli, as were actors Kris Kristofferson, Isabelle Huppert and Jeff Bridges. He exited the theatre just after the intermission, to make some furious phone calls – one to United Artists, demanding the film be pulled from release and not shown to anyone else until he and his editors (next on the list of urgent phone calls) could re-edit the film. But, by this time, the studio were so fed up with *Heaven's Gate* that they simply took control, radically editing it to the point where it barely made any linear sense whatsoever, and releasing it to theatres in a wildly truncated version that was choppy and meaningless. It ended up grossing less than $1 million at the domestic box-office. Cimino took the brunt of the ridicule and the criticism for what was seen as one of the biggest disasters in movie history.

It is with *Heaven's Gate* that the Mickey and Michael story begins. Rourke was cast in the film as the curiously named Nick Ray (recalling the director of classics like *Rebel without a Cause*), associate of plains hitman Nate Champion (Christopher Walken). Walken, Rourke's old Actor's Studio pal, was instrumental in getting him a meeting with Cimino. He strolled into Cimino's office and threw two handfuls of dirt onto the desk. Rourke explained that was how he saw the character, or the whole movie in fact – as down and dirty, of the land, a land that was forging a new era. Cimino liked his insolence, and his creative thinking, and instantly cast Rourke.

Even though his part was bigger in the original screenplay, the full-length version on DVD features an excised scene where Rourke is the butt of a practical joke by grimy muleskinner Geoffrey Lewis. The muleskinner tells Rourke's character he once fought off an angry wolf by grabbing its tongue. Rourke baulks at this, as the muleskinner shoots out a hand and grabs his tongue, urging Rourke to try to bite him. Of course he can't, with his tongue yanked on by the muleskinner's grimy fingers – much to the delight of Walken's character, who shakes with laughter.

Having been less than enthusiastic about his first experience of a big Hollywood extravaganza, Rourke was somewhat hesitant about going into another. But he was a great admirer of *The Deer Hunter*, and of Christopher Walken. 'I remember thinking that this little guy [Cimino] was so well organised,' said Rourke. 'He had this huge production going on all around him yet he could devote his absolute concentration on the smallest of details.' Rourke went on to explain, 'Even though my part was pretty small, I was still made to feel, by Michael, that it was an important part. He gave me direction – he wanted me to play this role very specifically so it would fit with the big vision he had for this film. I really responded well to that. I felt like I was really a part of this big story and that made me really want to give him everything I had.'

*Heaven's Gate* deserves to be looked at with fresh eyes and an open mind. It's a rich and complex film that is also beautiful to look at. The genius of cinematographer Vittorio Storaro is evident in every frame, shooting in golden-hued shades of sepia that evoke old photographs. The performances Cimino got from his cast were also first-rate, understated and thoughtful. From Kris Kristofferson, who gives the best performance of his entire career as James Averill – the cultured rich man who decided to give back to his country by becoming a lawman, siding with the dirt-poor citizens and against the people of his own class – to Jeff Bridges, who actually plays a character named Bridges who is an ancestor of the actor playing him. French actress Isabelle Huppert was given the female lead as the bordello madam who loves both Averill and Champion, over the vociferous objections of the studio. But Cimino insisted that Huppert's features, her accent, and the European style of naturalistic acting were perfect for this film.

*Heaven's Gate* is not a bad movie. It is certainly much maligned, and it would knock Cimino's career off the rails for years. (Even after he began working again, it would be his own obstinacy that would prove his biggest problem.)

French critics responded to the film quite differently to their American counterparts, as did French audiences. In France, the film was hailed as a near masterpiece, and one critic went so far as to predict that, one day, the Americans would take another look and it would gain a new-found respect.

For Mickey Rourke, *Heaven's Gate* would guarantee him (at the very least) a footnote in history as part of the cast of one of the most infamous films ever made. It would also connect him to a filmmaker he would form a lasting respect for, someone he would work with and return to on several occasions.

# Chapter Five

# MICKEY AT THE MOVIES

## '80 percent of success is just showing up.' – *Woody Allen*

When an actor starts getting heat around his name, there is a brighter, more intense light that shines upon him. And sometimes, when a hot young screenwriter decides it's time to make his directorial debut, he is occasionally afforded the leeway to cast the film. These elements came into play on the feature film that would put Mickey Rourke on the map – *Body Heat*.

Rourke has often stated openly that, without this film coming along at the right time, he would not have had the same career. 'I had only been in California for about six or seven months when I got the call to go in and read for *Body Heat*,' he said. 'They were offering me $500 a day for a couple of days work but I said to my agent that I wanted $1000 a day. He said, "Are you fucking kidding me? Every young actor in town is after this part."'

Rourke wasn't sure why he was making such a demand so early in his career, risking a great part for just a few extra bucks. But he was starting to understand the kind of people he would be constantly dealing with, if he were to stay in Hollywood. He was testing the waters of negotiation to see just how it all really worked.

*Body Heat* was written and directed by Lawrence Kasdan – a very hot young talent who moved quickly from writing ad copy at a PR firm to writing screenplays that got him big-time Hollywood assignments, like *The Empire Strikes Back* and *Raiders of the Lost Ark*. When he was given the chance to make a film as writer-director for the first time, he chose to explore a genre that had always been of interest to him as a movie fan – *film noir*.

In a very early draft of Kasdan's screenplay for *Body Heat*, the action was set in New Jersey. The move to a Florida location added infinitely to the impact of the film, the heat, humidity and sweat of the Gulf Coast oozing from every frame. It tells the story of Ned Racine (William Hurt), a small-town Florida lawyer constantly involved in random casual affairs with local women and tourists. One steamy night he involves himself with someone he thinks is yet another casual conquest, when he meets Mattie Walker (Kathleen Turner) at an outdoor concert. Even though she is married to a wealthy businessman, and openly tells Racine so, it doesn't seem to matter to him in the slightest. Mattie is a smoky-voiced, seemingly reluctant temptress, who confesses to Ned that she is always 'hot' because her body temperature perpetually runs a few degrees hotter than normal. After a thinly veiled invitation back to her house, the two fall into a torrid sex-

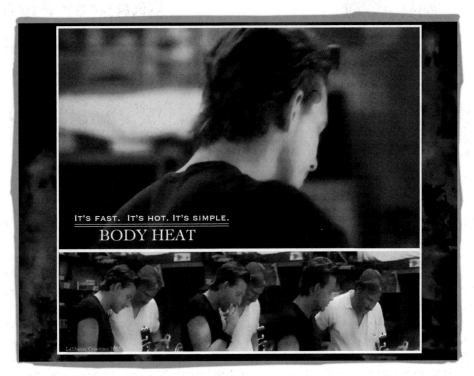

*This lobby card shows Rourke in his breakout film, as Teddy Lewis in* Body Heat *(1981). Male lead William Hurt is also seen, but Rourke blew him off the screen.*

ual affair. It intensifies rapidly and, before very long, each is telling the other that they cannot live without them, and they decide to kill her husband in a way that appears to be an accident. After doing the deed, Ned starts noticing both subtle and blatant hints that give him the queasy feeling he has been played all along. Before he can confirm it for himself, the whole sordid mess crumples on top of him, leaving Mattie to fly off to Rio with her dead husband's money and Ned to rot in a Florida prison cell.

The early draft of the screenplay had a title page that declared, 'BODY HEAT: An Original Screenplay' by Lawrence Kasdan. Indeed. The story has in fact been a staple of the *noir* genre since it began: The sad, repressed dame, the lovable schlub who falls victim to her sexual allure, as most men are wont to do, following her down a path he never would have travelled were he not under her erotic spell. Its archetypal depiction is in the novella *Double Indemnity* by James M. Cain, as directed for the screen by Billy Wilder. But still, Lawrence Kasdan's *Body Heat* is an earnest attempt at making classic *film noir* and, while it certainly looks and feels like the work of a first-time director, it remains effectively lush and lurid.

And it's also the film that announced how Mickey Rourke was going to be heard from in a big way, and made Kathleen Turner into one of the sexiest screen sirens in a couple of decades. It also established Kasdan as a director, even though his strength is in his screenwriting, his

**31**

direction having very little distinction in terms of personal style.

Rourke only appears in the film for two scenes, but he makes the absolute most of them. He plays a character named Teddy Lewis, an arsonist whom Ned Racine has kept out of prison via his legal representation. Ned goes to him for instruction on how to construct an incendiary device to cause a fire to cover up the murder he and Mattie are planning. We first see Rourke as Teddy, mouthing the words to a Bob Seger tune blaring in his workshop, as he watches Racine clumsily practising what he's been taught about wiring the device. Teddy grows frustrated with his ineptness and tries to talk him out of committing the crime in the first place. Rourke has a nice little moment in this first scene – he tells Hurt that the device has one major drawback, in that it's easy to spot and the fire will be deemed an arson almost immediately. Hurt shrugs this off, saying that it doesn't matter to him in the least. Rourke gives him a look of complete disbelief and incredulity that seems totally authentic.

The next time we see Rourke as Teddy, it is nearing the end of the film. Racine goes to visit him in lockdown after he's been picked up for questioning on an unrelated matter, but questions are asked about the arson-murder because it resembles his mode of operation. Teddy warns Ned that, while he has not talked yet, it's not something he can guarantee in the future, and that Ned should be careful because there are things about the investigation that he's not aware of.

Once again, Rourke makes this scene work, because of his jittery nervousness and honesty. You are seeing a guy react in a very natural way to these trying circumstances – he is not being a tough guy, or a hero, he is nervously trying to stay loyal to a friend while the pressure on him mounts.

Paul Newman once got a small role as a bartender in a play, and said that the way he approached the role was to make sure he was the best damn bartender any audience had ever seen. In *Body Heat*, Mickey Rourke didn't actually have a lot to do, but when he was on screen there was no one more important in the entire film. He only worked on the film for two days, but enjoyed the experience – as did Kasdan, who offered Rourke his next film, the Oscar-nominated breakthrough picture *The Big Chill*. (Rourke read the script through but then turned it down flat – 'the material just wasn't my cup of tea.')

*Body Heat* received a largely lukewarm critical reaction. One of the great American film critics, Pauline Kael, did not particularly like the film but singled out Rourke for praise. 'The actors in a few minor roles are considerably livelier,' she wrote in *The New Yorker*. 'And one, Mickey Rourke, who plays Teddy, a professional arsonist, has an awareness of danger that almost makes you feel that you are in a real movie.'

Rourke made a lasting impression by playing Teddy Lewis as a tough guy with a sense of honour, a blind loyalty towards anyone who has shown him such loyalty in the past. During the screening of the film that I caught when it was first released, I was sitting in front of a couple in their thirties who would make comments throughout. I remember the woman asking her male companion, 'Was that just an anal sex scene in a mainstream Hollywood movie?' (The dialogue exchanged by Ned and Mattie following the sex scene would seem to indicate it was.) Her next comment was, 'Have you ever seen that actor before, who is that?' when Rourke finished his first scene. That was my reaction too. After the screening I tried to find out what this guy Rourke had been in before, and what he was doing next.

*Body Heat* is a good little neo-*noir*. There is nothing particularly new about it that wasn't in countless old films before – with the exception of the nudity and the sex, which was not explicitly shown in comparison to latter-day films. Kathleen Turner was courageous when it came to baring herself emotionally and physically, but what got most of the audience talking, after the sex, was Mickey Rourke.

It was at this time that Rourke took the plunge into married life with Debra Feuer. He was filled with optimism and a feeling of sudden empowerment. His agent was now fielding offers without having to pitch his ass all over town. He had lucked into that piece of harmonic career convergence known as 'the breakout film'. But nothing was going to be more important than the first thing he did next, which would determine what kind of career he would have (or indeed, whether he continued to have a career at all).

For Rourke, *Diner* would be his second project in a row with a gifted writer making his first film as a director. In this case it was Barry Levinson, who would go on to establish himself as one of the most thoughtful and prolific A-list American filmmakers of his generation.

Already an award-winning writer, Levinson had decided to take a stab at directing one of his own scripts. Unlike Kasdan, he wanted to make a film that was based on things from his own life and upbringing. Levinson set *Diner* in his hometown of Baltimore, Maryland in 1959, the year he came of age. (He would go on to make several films set in Baltimore, either based on details from his own life or on characters and incidents that impacted on him while growing up.)

*Diner* concerns a group of young men who have been friends for many years, who meet for cherry Cokes and hamburgers at the Fells Point Diner, to talk about their lives and their frustrations. With hindsight, it seems a little rough to drop Mickey Rourke into a cast of young actors including Kevin Bacon, Steve Guttenberg, Paul Reiser and Daniel Stern. But into the mix he went, and once again he shone whenever he was onscreen. Rourke's character, Boogie Sheftell, was by far and away the most interesting of the group. Boogie's daytime job is as a hairdresser, while his evenings are spent taking law school courses. His other preoccupation is women, as many as he can get, as often as he can get them. All of the other guys have problems with their wives, or drinking, or self-esteem, but with Boogie it's gambling and he has racked up a massive debt to a local bookie.

The dialogue is clever and the characters finely etched, the many memorable set-pieces gaining Levinson an Academy Award nomination for his screenplay. The most memorable scene of the film takes place in a darkened movie theatre, where Boogie has taken a snobbish but not too bright young woman to see *A Summer Place*. Boogie has bet his pals that he can get this girl, whom he has just met, to 'go for his pecker' on their first date. He comes up with a scheme to stick his penis through an opening he has crafted in his popcorn box, so that when the girl reaches for a handful of popcorn Boogie will have won the wager. The scene turns even funnier when Boogie concocts a completely asinine excuse to explain to this girl how the whole thing was nothing more than an accident.

*Diner* doesn't really have a story per se, but it simply and effectively weaves together a series of episodes into a well-arranged patchwork. Watching *Diner* is probably more fun if you grew up in the era that the film is set in. But even though a number of the cast went on to careers

*In* Diner, *Rourke's understated performance stole the film from co-stars (left to right) Kevin Bacon, Daniel Stern and Timothy Daly.*

as working actors, even stars, their contributions to this film were not all that stellar: Paul Reiser went on to major success with his TV show *Mad About You*, but has pretty much played himself in everything he has done; Ellen Barkin, one of the female supports in *Diner*, went on to a solid career as a character actress playing sultry bad girls, but in this film she seemed to have no confidence in her own abilities (something she obviously got over). But Rourke got the best deal, not least because Boogie was the most idiosyncratic of the main characters. He read his material well, and while the other cast members were chewing scenery and going wildly over the top, he underplayed his scenes and drew even more attention as the quiet, mysterious character who haunts the movie even when he's not on screen.

As with a lot of the films that Rourke would make, after he completed his work problems began arising. The studio backing the film, MGM, did so with the expectation that they were getting in on the wave of lowball comedy hits like *National Lampoon's Animal House* or the wildly successful Canadian exploitation hit *Porky's*. Brainless gross-out comedy filled with juvenile sex jokes, in other words. What they got was a talky, quite funny, but ultimately clever little film about the passage of time, and the effect it has on a group of guys blindsided by change and fighting the notion of growing up.

It left MGM in a quandary. The cut of the film that Levinson delivered was simply not what the marketing department were prepared to sell to the public. They decided to try test screenings, but the cards filled out by the audiences proved utterly inconclusive. The decision was made to dump the film in a few theatres here and there (a theatrical release of at least one week contractually guaranteed to Levinson) and then just add it to the long list of films that the studio wrote off.

Barry Levinson was crushed by this decision. He took the bold step of surreptitiously arranging a screening of the film in New York, eliciting a slew of rave reviews, enhanced by the story of a big Hollywood studio stomping on the earnest efforts of a filmmaker who poured heart and soul into his film. MGM turned around and used this newly acquired buzz to re-open the film, garnering Oscar nominations and adding to the momentum that Mickey Rourke's career was gathering.

His next role was an important one in the transition from screen actor to screen icon. Two female fans of his, both successful women, have told me without prompting that they have been in love with Rourke 'ever since *Rumble Fish*'.

In the early Eighties, director Francis Ford Coppola was trying to shift gears. He had been through the experience of making the first two *Godfather* films, and all the glory and accolades that attached themselves to two American classics. Then he went through the gruelling, nightmarish experience of the flawed masterpiece *Apocalypse Now*, and the failure of his revisionist Hollywood musical *One from the Heart*. After all that, he was trying to go down to a place that was less all-consuming of both resources and emotions. Coppola wanted to get back to being a filmmaker and get away from being an event maker. And from Rourke's perspective, meeting and working with Coppola would be one of the most fortuitous things that ever happened to him.

Coppola had purchased the rights to a couple of thin young adult novels by S. E. (Susie) Hinton that he wanted to quickly make into two low-budget films on location. They would be inexpensive enough to allow him to experiment with different filmmaking techniques, and a mixture of fresh new actors alongside older veteran performers. The first of these was *The Outsiders*, a film about juvenile delinquency in Tulsa, Oklahoma, that would feature such new young actors as Tom Cruise, Emilio Estevez, Patrick Swayze and Ralph Macchio. At the time he was casting this film, Coppola also saw the young Mickey Rourke. As much as he liked Rourke, there was no role that he could see the actor fitting comfortably into. But Coppola filed Rourke away under *Rumble Fish*, the Hinton novel he would tackle right after *The Outsiders*.

I asked Coppola about this early contact with Rourke on a sunny afternoon in Cannes. 'I saw a lot of actors during this time,' he said. 'A lot of them were terrific and really went on to prove themselves, some were not so great, and then there was Mickey Rourke. Right away I saw something interesting in this guy, something exotic about this guy, something that I wanted to use, but I didn't know how or where because my head was still deep into *The Outsiders,* but once I started thinking about *Rumble Fish* I knew that I would write the Motorcycle Boy character around Mickey Rourke and see where we could go with that.'

*The Outsiders* was successful enough to make the Hollywood bean counters relax and green-light *Rumble Fish*. But this film would be a departure, a moody look at disenfranchised people on the fringes of society, and how they actually evolve into an alternative society of their own – with their own rules and laws, their own little system of checks and balances. The film was shot in atmospherically rich black and white, with the exception of a few startling splashes of colour for effect. This immediately put it outside the parameters of what most North American film audiences had become accustomed to. Allegory and metaphor were also very much a part of the fabric of the film. Glances at clocks on the wall that have no hands, images of clouds whizzing by at an accelerated speed giving an altered perception of time. Time slipping away is the central theme of the film.

The story is of a young man named Rusty James (Matt Dillon) who, after years of idolising his older brother (Rourke), is now dangerously disengaged. His brother, known only as the Motorcycle Boy, has left town as part of a truce reached by two rival street gangs. The Motorcycle Boy becomes legendary in his absence, a legend out of proportion with the reality of a deeply disturbed young man slowly losing his grip on sanity. When he returns to town, Rusty sees his life as getting back on track because his hero brother is now there to guide him. But the Motorcycle Boy is not in a position to guide or counsel anyone about anything. And as this realisation dawns on Rusty, his entire little fabricated community begins to come apart at the seams.

*Rumble Fish* holds a deep significance for Rourke that extends beyond his career. There was a depth of feeling to the material that increased considerably while the film was being made, when Mickey's beloved half-brother Joey made the frightening discovery that he had cancer. This first bout (there would sadly be many) was a nasty one, taking Joey right to the edge of death before lessening its grip.

Another deeply affecting aspect to the shoot was the coincidental convergence between his relationship with his onscreen father (played by Dennis Hopper) and the lack thereof with his own father. In the film, the Motorcycle Boy and his father have a distant, indifferent relationship. Rourke built his similar feelings into that characterisation, and was reaching out to his father in the way that the Motorcycle Boy reached out to his. Then, in a sadly ironic twist, word arrived at the set in Tulsa that Mickey's father was dying, and was not expected to last very much longer.

'There was this whole identity thing going on – who was my father?' said Rourke. 'We were just starting to get to know one another, as men, adults, I started to write to him and I was planning to arrange for him to come and visit. All of a sudden I had lost the opportunity to be buddies with him. It was too late. And while it was too late for me, it was also too late for the Motorcycle Boy as well. It was a very painful thing and I started feeling like there was no reason for me to be sticking around anymore, it was a really painful time and I used that in the film.'

When Coppola began adapting the novel into screenplay form he did so with a great deal of licence – he especially took liberties with the character of the Motorcycle Boy. Coppola based his description of the character partly on Rourke himself, and in part on pictures he had seen of the French existentialist writer Albert Camus. Rourke's hairstyle in the film was based on the style sported by Camus, and he was instructed to hold his cigarette in the same manner that Camus did in the photos.

Rourke remembers the shooting of the film as being somewhat surreal. 'Francis was directing the film largely from inside a trailer using a PA system to give direction. He had Stewart Copeland [the percussionist for The Police and the music composer for the film] sitting beside him beating on the drums to create a rhythm for the scene, it was trippy,' said Rourke. 'He was experimenting with directing without actually being on the set and he was using all these weird

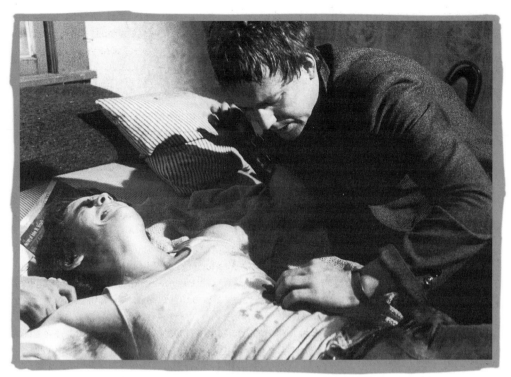

*The Motorcycle Boy (Rourke) aids his brother, Rusty James (Matt Dillon), after injury in a gang fight.*
Rumble Fish *(1983) coincided with personal sadness in Rourke's own life.*

metaphors so most of the time I didn't know what the fuck he was talking about. But I never had a director talk to me the way that Francis did before – it was very cool. I really respected that.'

I had the opportunity to ask actor Matt Dillon about his experiences on *Rumble Fish*. 'I was really excited about doing this film with Francis,' said Dillon. 'I had worked on *The Outsiders* with him and saw, and felt, how he was really trying to expand the boundaries of American film – he was into experimenting and re-thinking and trying to go against the grain. I was really excited to be a part of that, I wish there were more guys out there like him.' And Rourke? 'I thought Mickey Rourke was the coolest fucking guy in the world,' said Dillon. 'And he had that special kind of cool, that kind of very un-Hollywood cool. In LA every asshole pretends to be a badass and pretends to be cool – but most of them are nothing but Hollywood pussies – Mickey is cool without trying, he didn't need to posture – he was just a cool guy.'

*Rumble Fish* got a rather rough ride from most mainstream critics and, this time, Rourke was not spared their wrath. Oddly, some bellowed that he was entirely unsuited for his role in this down and dirty street version of *Hamlet*. More still found his performance pretentious and steeped in obvious technique. But such is the way with critics: the vast majority of whom have never made a film themselves, and always harp on about how no fresh ideas come out of Hollywood.

Rourke had gone with Coppola all the way on this stuff – he played his character as a James

Dean figure, someone who seems like the very personification of cool, while at the same time harbouring deep psychological problems. It makes him completely unable to deal with the way people position him on a pedestal because, while he enjoys the esteem, he is completely unable to comprehend where it comes from.

The Motorcycle Boy has some terrific lines of dialogue in the film ('If you are going to lead people, you have to have somewhere to go') and Rourke's readings added to the impact. He spoke in that wonderful whisper that is three parts sensitive human being and one part tightly-wound malevolent force.

The first part of the film is slightly awkward, because the early scenes feel like they belong to a different, lighter toned movie. But the way Coppola develops his characters, each one having a distinct style of dress and a particular way of moving, makes the movie consistently interesting. It is not a classic by any stretch of the imagination, but *Rumble Fish* is much more engaging and entertaining than *The Outsiders.* Author Susie Hinton has enthused publicly that, '*Rumble Fish* is one of those strange movies that you either love it or you hate it . . . and I love it . . . . Francis Coppola really understood the book, but he also stayed true to his own vision. It is his movie.'

Mickey Rourke was now entering that strange place where celebrity status changes everything. Interview requests, meetings with filmmakers and studios who wanted to work with the hot new actor were all coming fast and furiously. He was struggling to keep his equilibrium. 'Success did change him,' said his wife of the time, Debra Feuer. 'It brought out the best of him and the worst of him. But anyone out there who thinks they are immune to such changes when they happen so big and so fast are just fooling themselves.'

He was not yet at the stage where people made career decisions for him based on the size of their percentage of his salary. So Rourke was still free to look at everything and talk to anyone – including the iconoclastic British filmmaker Nicolas Roeg. Roeg had already dazzled audiences with such brilliant films as *Performance*, *Walkabout*, the hauntingly mesmerising *Don't Look Now*, *The Man Who Fell to Earth* and *Bad Timing*. Singularly strange in his vision, his films were all possessed of an intelligence that ensured they would never fall into the category of weirdness for its own sake. Despite their tilt towards surrealism, they never became otherworldly or inaccessible. The film Roeg wanted to discuss with Rourke was a complicated tale of single-minded determination and desire, followed by the destructive power of greed, to be called *Eureka*. Rourke and Roeg had actually started talking about this film before *Diner* had arrived in theatres, so the actor was in a different place, professionally speaking, when it finally became time to shoot. But Rourke is a loyal guy. When he commits to someone or something, he will follow through unless the most extreme circumstances prevent it.

The character Rourke was to play was a well-dressed gangster named Aurelio D'Amato, who does the bidding for a Jewish gang boss named Mayakofsky. The film itself is about a prospector in the 1920s who, after fifteen hard years of searching, finally strikes gold – so much gold that it elevates him to the position of one of the richest men on earth, almost instantly. The story then jumps ahead twenty years and the prospector, Jack McCann (Gene Hackman), lives on his own island in the Caribbean, surrounded by (as Hunter S. Thompson called them) greed-heads. His wife is a bored alcoholic. His daughter is a materialistic brat married to a ridiculously obvious social climber, and, to add intrigue to the mix, McCann is under siege from gangsters who insist on buying his island to develop into a little Cuba, filled with nightclubs and casinos. So Jack has fulfilled his dream after years of toil, only to find in subsequent years that it has done nothing but bring him heartache and very little peace of mind.

Making *Eureka* granted Rourke the opportunity to work with Hackman, an actor of the highest calibre who he had always admired (and who had also shifted furniture at the same warehouse where Rourke once worked). It also meant he would get to spend the latter part of 1981 and the early part of 1982 on location in the Caribbean (the film was shot in Jamaica, Florida, Vancouver and England), and to play a smart guy in tailored suits for a change. The film would also feature Dutch actor Rutger Hauer (who would later play a small role in *Sin City*) and the sexy-voiced actress Theresa Russell, who was married to Roeg during this time.

*Eureka* is not up there with Roeg's best work, but it is certainly worth a look. (It was released for mass consumption on DVD in 2003.) For reasons that have a lot to do with bad marketing, it sat on the shelf for a couple of years after it was finished and finally made it onto a few screens in 1984. The theatrical release box-office returns are listed as less than $100,000.

For Mickey Rourke this film is something of a curiosity, in that he does not make an appearance in it until almost half the running time has elapsed and his role is not all that deep or consequential to the overall story. He took it for the opportunity to go on location and work with some interesting people. (It's always refreshing when you ask an actor or director why they did a particular project, and you get an honest answer: 'I wanted to hang out in Italy,' or, 'I needed the money.') He holds his own in the scenes that he appears in, but this is far from his best work either.

And as strange as it may seem, Rourke was already feeling the first major pangs of disillusionment with his Hollywood career. Sure, he liked the money and the attention, but the amount of stress and bullshit that seemed to be connected with every film he made was starting to weigh heavily on him.

# Chapter Six

# ICONIC MEASURES

## 'I can resist anything but temptation.' – *Oscar Wilde*

Mickey Rourke has said in the past that the film that sealed his conviction to give up acting, and return to the ring, was *Harley Davidson and the Marlboro Man.* But if we probe a bit deeper, we find that after making one of his best loved films, *The Pope of Greenwich Village*, his interest in being a movie actor began to wane.

   *The Pope of Greenwich Village* was taken from the novel of the same name by Vincent Patrick, who also adapted his book into a screenplay. It tells the story of two cousins from the old neighbourhood in New York City, the area around Carmine Street in Little Italy – Charlie Moran (Rourke) is the older, wiser, and more headstrong of the two, while Paulie Giboni (Eric Roberts) is a more fancy-free dreamer.

   One night, both lose their jobs at the same restaurant because Paulie has been skimming off the top on large orders, and Charlie, as his cousin, was believed to be in on it by familial association. Charlie has an ex-wife to whom he is paying support payments, a little son he is supporting, and a few 'shylocks' (loan sharks) he is carrying. Paulie has no such responsibilities, but he too is up to his neck in loan shark debt. He digs an even deeper hole by borrowing another five grand from the shylocks, to buy a third of a racehorse and put into motion his plan of a big dream score by robbing a local trucking company. Charlie's big dream is of getting out of the city and owning a nice little country restaurant. But with no job, and no real prospects, Charlie is lured against his better judgement into going along with Paulie on the ill-planned robbery, together with an old Bronx locksmith named Barney (nicely played by the late Kenneth Macmillan) as their safecracker.

   A subplot emerges that involves a Mob boss named Bedbug Eddie Grant (played with burly, thuggish menace by Burt Young) and his arrangement with a squad of corrupt New York City detectives. When the robbery was being planned, the one thing Paulie forgot to tell his partners was that the trucking company belonged to Bedbug Eddie, and the cash they take from the safe was intended to pay off the bent detectives – one of whom is accidentally killed when he surprises them during the robbery, and falls down an elevator shaft. Paulie, Charlie and Barney are despondent, but decide to continue with the robbery anyway ('it don't change the beef none one way or the other'). But they are doing it under the crushing weight of the knowledge that they are now essentially cop killers.

When Bedbug Eddie gets wind of the robbery, he flies into a rage. He has heard tell that Paulie Giboni from Carmine Street might be involved and, because Paulie's uncle Pete (Tony Musante) is part of Eddie's crew, he puts him in charge of getting to the bottom of it. Pete confirms that Paulie was involved and, in a gesture of brutal street justice, is sent to visit Paulie with two goons to exact revenge. The thugs cut one of Paulie's thumbs off with a pocketknife.

Charlie, who is still unknown to Bedbug Eddie, decides to avenge his cousin's torture by revealing to Eddie that he took a tape from a concealed tape recorder on the body of the dead cop, which has some damning criminal evidence relating to Bedbug and his arrangements. Charlie's actions are spurred on by the fact that his girlfriend has just revealed she is pregnant – and has taken his shoebox full of loot from the robbery, so that she and the baby can have a good start away from the criminal atmosphere.

But all is not completely bleak for the cousins – Paulie's racehorse, Starry Hope, comes in second in her first race, netting Charlie a cool twenty grand after he bets on her across the board.

Charlie confronts Bedbug Eddie, in a tense standoff at the private club where Paulie is forced to work as a coffee boy as further penance for his crime: 'This may be your church, but right now I am the Pope of Greenwich Village . . . 'cause I got a tape!' While Bedbug Eddie is distracted by Charlie, Paulie fills his espresso with lye – causing the Bedbug's throat to disintegrate the second he throws back his drink. Charlie and Paulie escape in the commotion and beat a hasty path out of town – all to the strains of Frank Sinatra's 'The Summer Wind'.

The gestation period of *The Pope of Greenwich Village* was a big money snakes and ladders game that involved several different cast changes, until, almost despite itself, the film finally got made. Originally it was planned as the first onscreen pairing of Al Pacino and Robert De Niro, with De Niro playing Charlie and Pacino as Paulie. Two of the most accomplished actors of their generation, both were also known as finicky professionals, and changes to the script were insisted upon by both. After a while the timing of the project became an issue, and De Niro was the first to back out, citing commitment to another film.

Pacino was still in the cast when Mickey Rourke was approached about playing the vacated Charlie Moran role. Rourke was thrilled at the prospect of working with Pacino, an actor he had admired from the back of the training room in the Actor's Studio just a few years before. But now it was Pacino's turn to show some hesitancy. He reread the material and decided that the new dynamic didn't really work with him in the Paulie role, as he was older than Rourke, who was playing the more dominant, in-control character.

Rourke looked at it from a different perspective, believing it would add a depth and poignancy to the story. As he told me, 'You know, there is something pathetic and sad about a younger guy having to take care of an older relative like that. But on the other hand there is also something endearing about that too, and Pacino is one actor who could have pulled off that balance brilliantly.'

The offer went out to another very hot actor of the day, the gangly, expressive Eric Roberts, who made a very interesting (albeit not widely seen) screen debut at 22 in the 1978 film *King of the Gypsies*. He would go on to be nominated for Golden Globes and Oscars for his work in such films as *Star 80* and *Runaway Train.* Rourke was quite an admirer of Roberts' work, and was thrilled when he signed on to play Paulie.

With the two leads now signed, the scheduled director, Michael Cimino, wanted to finesse the screenplay with some rewriting and restructuring. But what Cimino wanted to do would take him over the mandated start date for shooting. The studio panicked, and Cimino and MGM parted company. Journeyman director Stuart Rosenberg stepped into the breach.

As much as Rourke liked Rosenberg, he was equally thrilled at first by the prospect of working with Cimino again. But MGM, the backers, were now called MGM/UA, as they had absorbed the studio the director was accused of bankrupting. The spectre of it all still haunted the famously timid executives. Cimino also nearly directed *Footloose*, but once again parted ways with the studio for similar reasons.

Stuart Rosenberg was born in 1927, and began his career in 1955 in New York City. Starting out in live TV, he would spend the next few years honing his skills in episodic series (including directing three episodes of the classic *Twilight Zone*). Rosenberg would win an Emmy Award for his direction of the television series *The Defenders*, before heading into feature films. In 1967 he would direct the classic *Cool Hand Luke*, and in 1979 he made the original version of *The Amityville Horror* – an enormous hit that was, for a while, the highest grossing non-studio American film ever. Rosenberg liked the Vincent Patrick novel and liked the screenplay of *The Pope of Greenwich Village* even more. He was further enthused by exploring the combination of Mickey Rourke and Eric Roberts as his lead actors. As Rosenberg said at the time, 'Together they are fascinating. You get the whole spectrum when the two of them are together – in their physical attributes, emotions, and approaches. They're sympathetic guys whom the audience sides with immediately. They broadcast their fears and their desires and their vulnerabilities so cleverly that the audiences forgive them no matter what they do.'

But the acting styles of Rourke and Roberts are completely different, and would have proved daunting to a director with less confidence and experience. Rosenberg embraced those differences and put them to work for the good of the project. 'They are total opposites in that respect,' he said. 'Mickey is a street kid, tough, unpolished, but with an ingenious quality that I hadn't seen since John Garfield stopped making movies. As an actor he plays it completely off the cuff – changes lines from take to take, used whatever was going on around him.'

Roberts, on the other hand, was a lot more studious and precise. He prepared himself very carefully and delivered his lines exactly as written. When he was asked about the wide gap in their work ethics at the time, Roberts' response was unexpectedly generous. 'Mickey would arrive on the set looking like he had just crawled out of bed and croak, "What scene are we shooting today?" I'd tell him and he would just wander away. But he is great – the most naturalistic actor I have ever worked with. His style didn't bother me at all, it was what ended up on screen that counted and I knew, I could tell instinctually that it was good stuff.'

Rourke, for his part, always sang Roberts' praises. He later remarked to me how he was saddened by the fact that he and Roberts never found the opportunity to work together again, especially since the pair had planned a number of different projects over the years. At the time they were making *The Pope of Greenwich Village*, Rourke said of his acting partner, 'Eric is so giving. He is there. We work off each other so well, and there is a lot of love there, which is what this

*Rourke as Charlie in* The Pope of Greenwich Village *(1984), with Daryl Hannah as his girl and Eric Roberts as Paulie. Despite box-office failure, the film now has iconic status.*

movie is really all about. It's a love story. Charlie would rather be with Paulie than with his girl.'

Once the film was fully cast and shooting began, Rourke and Roberts gelled beautifully. Their scenes together had a resonance and a spark. 'I loved working with Eric Roberts, really, he is one of the best actors I have ever worked with and I would have been happy to have worked with him on ten movies in a row,' said Rourke later. Among their list of aborted potential projects would be a Western based on the lives of Frank and Jesse James, which would have been a joy to watch. But the pair would be seen on screen together again only briefly, for a couple of moments in the 2002 film *Spun*.

Apart from the joy of working with Roberts, the role of Charlie Moran led to Rourke remaking himself physically. He put on some pounds so he would look like a guy who enjoyed his food, his restaurants and his soft life. After playing Charlie, Mickey quickly shucked off the excess weight and cut and dyed his hair bright orange. As he said at the time, 'I feel that I am a very lucky man. A lot of anger that I used to walk around with is now gone. I can channel it constructively, which makes it a lot easier for the people in my life like Stuart Rosenberg, Sandra Seacat, and my wife.'

Where his marriage was concerned, Rourke's newfound fame and fortune caused some strange behaviour. Not that he turned his back on his wife, Debra Feuer. He bought her a house – not a house for the both of them, but just for Debra. He took a lease out on a penthouse suite at the Mayflower Hotel in New York City. He bought Debra a nice car. He bought himself a few luxury cars and a Harley Davidson motorcycle *and* an Airstream trailer, to use as his combined home and office while he was on the road. The marriage took place at long distance, unconventional almost from day one.

'I had a thing with my wife about hotels,' said Rourke shortly afterward. 'I had to make a decision as to what my priorities were. And besides that, I tend towards getting self destructive in New York City. Whatever schedule I put together, I just can't seem to stick to because I am having too much fun.'

Part of that fun lay in having affairs with a number of women, something that would ultimately cause an irreparable rift in the marital relationship. 'He was like Jekyll and Hyde,' said Feuer, 'he really took to the attention and the money.'

During this time, Rourke had a very public dalliance with actor/model Lauren Hutton, who had starred with Richard Gere in *American Gigolo*. The pair were seen publicly everywhere together – at events, at restaurants, they even gave a couple of joint interviews. And on one occasion they were involved in a car wreck that destroyed Rourke's Mercedes Benz (while his wife was at the house he bought her, waiting for him to arrive).

Career-wise, things seemed to be going great, and Rourke believed that *The Pope of Greenwich Village* would be a huge hit. But it was at this point that disappointment and disillusionment started to set in. Once it was had been through postproduction and editing, MGM just dumped it into theatres with little or no fanfare. The studio was going through one of its many regime changes, and *The Pope of Greenwich Village* was caught in the middle of this interoffice politics. This was not the MGM of the Golden Age of Hollywood, and they completely sabotaged the film with an inept, inappropriate marketing campaign.

When the film finally hit the theatres, it was only a very moderate hit with the critics. Critical opinion seems to have become more buoyantly enthusiastic with the passing of time, but back then film critic, Pauline Kael, called it a 'moderately entertaining bad movie'. And the movie failed to gain any kind of audience at all, largely because of the dismissive way that the studio treated it.

Rourke, Roberts and Rosenberg were all taken completely aback – all thought they had delivered some of the strongest work they had ever done. And Rourke sang the praises of the film at the top of his lungs when it was released, whereas his later bad reputation would stem in part from how he was more than willing to criticise his own films, if he thought they deserved it. He was particularly effusive in his praise for the director: 'Francis Coppola is a god. He can do anything. Stuart is the same way. Stuart Rosenberg is a genius. I want to do ten movies with him because I have never liked doing anything as much as I enjoyed *The Pope of Greenwich Village*.'

During the making of the film, Rourke had also connected with an older guy who would become a friend and confidant. He was one of the actors who played the thugs who removed Paulie's thumb, and his name was Leonard Termo. His craggy face would appear alongside Rourke again in small parts in *Year of the Dragon*, *A Prayer for the Dying* and *Barfly*, as well as in *Fight Club*, *Ed Wood*, *Godzilla* and *Ali*, to name a few. Rourke seems to gravitate towards older men for his closest friendships, almost as if they're filling the substantial gap left by the absence of his father. Stuart Rosenberg was another who Rourke took to very easily. As Debra Feuer would say, 'A lot of directors that Mickey enjoyed working with were really father figures to him.'

*The Pope of Greenwich Village* is one of the best films of Mickey Rourke, and holds up well against the test of time. The lush dialogue and the story remain interesting even on repeated viewing, as do the interesting little nuances in the performances of Rourke and Roberts.

Rourke was entirely correct when he called the film a love story – albeit a much more complex love story than most. As a crime drama it works well because of the subtlety of how it unfolds. This is not a bang-bang action film, dealing instead with the grey areas of law and order and street life in New York City. Irish cops are in bed with Italian Mafia guys. Half-Irish guys live with blonde white women (Charlie's girlfriend is played by Daryl Hannah, the only weak actor in the film, cast because of her long lean body rather than her thespian skills), while supporting their Italian ex-wives. But there is nothing that the main characters could do that you would not forgive them for, which is illustrative of the dimensions that the writing gives them.

*The Pope of Greenwich Village* is truly a classic example of how a good film, with real box-office potential, can be completely shipwrecked by a bewildering lack of commitment from the studio that made it. If the studio is not willing to get behind the film and support it, then why should the paying public?

By the time Mickey Rourke and Michael Cimino worked together again, Rourke was credited above the title as the star of the film. MGM/UA was the studio once again, but, in the case of *Year of the Dragon*, it was the buccaneering spirit of famed producer Dino De Laurentiis that raised most of the money. To maintain a semblance of control, he insisted that the film, set in New York City, be shot at his own studios in North Carolina. He was hopeful that Cimino would deliver another *Deer Hunter*, rather than waltzing into another *Heaven's Gate*.

Rourke was very keen on working with Cimino, but was not initially all that approving of the script. 'I don't think I would have done *Year of the Dragon* if it was sent to me by anyone else but Michael Cimino,' he said. 'There is what is on the page and then there is what is on the page plus what a good director will give you on top of that. Michael Cimino is one of those good directors who will always give you more than you see going in.' Or, as he later put it, 'As long as I am working with Michael Cimino I would be happy to play a monkey, I would do anything for that guy.'

*Year of the Dragon* is based on the novel of the same name by Robert Daley, telling the factually-based story of a decorated New York City cop named Stanley White. Fact and fiction merge in the use of White's real name, and the depiction of a real-life turf war involving powerful Chinese Triad gangs. But it remains a novel, not a biographical treatment of White's life and career.

In both the novel and the film White is transferred to the Chinatown area, where his real-life counterpart made it his life's mission to do battle with the Asian organised crime gangs. But he ran into a huge wall of resistance when it came to dealing with the centuries-old traditions of bribe paying and extortion. With dubious ethics, White enlisted the help of an attractive TV newswoman, and actually did make an impact on Chinatown by causing problems for one of its biggest players, a suave Hong Kong gangster called Joey Tai. But these gains came at a very high price for White and the officers who joined his fight – including his own wife's murder by Chinese gang punks seeking revenge, and the death of a young Chinese undercover officer thrust into the line of duty before his training was complete.

The screenplay assignment was handed to a hot young writer named Oliver Stone, who had won the Oscar for writing the factually based but sensationalised *Midnight Express*, and also wrote the highly controversial remake of *Scarface*. (Stone was still a year away from writing and directing his definitive work, the autobiographical *Platoon*.) Cimino would give the script a rewrite before shooting began, but by this point there was significant contention over the project as a whole. The Stone screenplay met with howls of protest from the Asian community, accusing him of abject racism and unfairly contributing to the stereotyping of an entire community. In one of the most interesting public exchanges during this heated debate, Stone answered criticism by saying, 'He knows shit about Chinese people or Chinatown, his criticism is invalid and bullshit and it means nothing to me.' The 'he' that Stone was referring to was award-winning Chinese-American filmmaker Wayne Wang.

De Laurentiis had told Cimino that he would be on a short but flexible leash. Apart from constructing his sets on De Laurentiis' back lot at his North Carolina studios (which Cimino arranged so brilliantly that even Stanley Kubrick publicly remarked at how amazed he was with the results), Cimino would shoot in the relatively inexpensive locations of Vancouver and Thailand.

Whatever his personal demons, whatever his ego and control issues, Cimino embraced the opportunity. To hear him tell the story in the rather odd and rambling commentary he provides on the DVD version of the film, he was actually quite resistant to the project, and had to be offered it several times by De Laurentiis because he thought the story was overly violent for violence's sake. Once Stone came up with a draft that was still violent but did not overwhelm the story or the motivations of the characters, Cimino signed on.

Rourke was initially interested in the story, but was confused as to why he was being offered the Stanley White character, who was written as being at least fifteen years older than him. 'They had to break a lot of stuff down for me,' he said at the time. 'Most of it was physical. This guy walked the straight and narrow, if someone did something wrong, this cop was on them in two seconds – I needed to find a way to translate that attitude into the physical presentation of the character and that took me a while to sort out.'

Rourke gave a lot of credit to Cimino for his creation of his character. He had become used to using his soft voice to project an understated menace, but Cimino had something else in mind, a different kind of pacing. He knew that if Rourke was playing a New York City police captain, he simply needed to project enough authority to make the performance authentic. Cimino suggested Rourke add weight to his frame, so that when he walked into a scene he did so with a burly physical bluster, and also that he sneer and rant out his lines with an anger that spat the words at the other characters.

The shooting progressed well. Rourke and Cimino had found a dynamic working rhythm, and a young Asian actor named John Lone delivered a career-making performance as Joey Tai. (Lone would go on to star in Bertolucci's multi-Oscar-winning *The Last Emperor*.) And perhaps

*Uncompromising NYPD cop Stanley White (Rourke) goes eye to eye with Triad gangster Joey Tai (John Lone), in Michael Cimino's* Year of the Dragon *(1985).*

most significantly, Cimino brought this complex film in on time and on budget.

In the days leading up to the release of the film, there was a lot of controversy surrounding the accusations of racism, or the anticipated return of Michael Cimino from the ashes of his former self. The racial controversy got so intense that it was agreed upon to open with an onscreen disclaimer proclaiming the film as a depiction of a small segment of the Asian community, not a reflection of the community as a whole. There were other criticisms that were heaped on the film too. Much was made of the fact that the year the film came out, 1985, was not the Year of the Dragon at all, but the Year of the Ox. But nowhere in the film does it say it is actually set in 1985, so that particular criticism was meaningless. It was also stated by those supposedly in the know that the idea of the Chinese gangs hustling their way across Canal Street, into the territory long controlled by the Italian Mafia, was not only pure invention but could never be taken seriously. As it turned out, that aspect of the story would prove rather prophetic – in the battles for territorial superiority of the early Nineties, the Mafia would try to fight off not only the Hong Kong Triad gangs, but also gangs of Vietnamese and Russian origin as well.

One of the most enduring criticisms levelled at *Year of the Dragon* was purely aesthetic. It concerned Rourke's hair, and the fact that it seemed to change colour from sequence to sequence. In one scene it would be all grey, almost white, while in the very next it would be only grey around the temples, turning a kind of iron grey in the scene after that. It's bewildering, given Cimino's famous attention to detail. But Rourke was whitening or greying his hair as a shortcut to depicting the age difference between his character and himself, which was in part his idea. As he said, 'I didn't want to go in for the applied wrinkles kind of thing. I was more interested in the fact that this guy had been around death for so long, not willingly, not because he wanted it or liked it, but because he was a Vietnam vet and a street cop. I wanted that to be reflected physically somehow, so you could see how drained he was, I figured that since he had faced death prematurely that it would make him older prematurely, older looking.'

Cimino had pretty much decided that Rourke was the only guy for the role of Stanley White. Part of what Cimino liked about him was his boxer's carriage and demeanour. Cimino wanted Rourke bulked up, but also in top physical condition. He arrived in a somewhat lesser state, bulked up but soft around the edges. So much so that Cimino arranged a rather unorthodox trainer for Rourke: a member of the Hells Angels motorcycle club, who had developed a rigorous and effective physical training programme while in prison.

Rourke decided to forego the Stanley White character that Robert Daley had loosely fictionalised in his book, and go directly to the real White. Rourke is known for his instinctual preparation rather than any specific hands-on research, but in this case he felt it needed something different. At this time White was attached to the Los Angeles Country Sheriff's Department, and Rourke would go out with him on over 30 homicide calls. He found himself growing more and more comfortable with the role as his research progressed. Rourke also noticed that White had a couple of tattoos: one was a scale of justice, with a skull and the number 187 inside it (the numerical California penal code for murder); the other was on his right shoulder and depicted a clown's head. Rourke decided he wanted a tattoo as a souvenir of the film, and chose a leopard head with the Chinese ideogram representing the Year of the Dragon inside it. He also sought out an NYPD detective named John Fusano, who worked out of the Fifth District (Chinatown), and hung out with him to research more specifics. Once again, Detective Fusano would allow Rourke to go out on calls with him, and even introduced him to some real Asian gang leaders without letting on that he was an actor researching a role.

Rourke was excited about the film and his work in it. Unusually effusive in his support, he even kept an office full of promotional items to give away – including posters and cool long sleeved t-shirts with *Year of the Dragon* written on the front and 'Cimino Is Back' across the back.

'I was sure the movie would be a big hit,' said Rourke. 'And I was sure that Cimino would be completely redeemed because of it, but in this business just being good ain't nearly good enough most of the time, you also have to be lucky.' The film marked one of those rare occasions in Mickey Rourke's career when he actually cared about the potential box office returns.

Rourke was beginning to be concerned about his continued commercial viability, worried that he was only making movies that 'about six people are going to see'. So when the film was trashed by critics, and met with utter indifference from audiences, Rourke was profoundly disappointed. He himself was treated mostly fairly in the reviews, but Cimino predictably became the target for all sorts of critical vitriol.

Critic John Simon was one of the most scathing of the film's detractors. 'The whole thing is such a crashing waste, and not a little racist to boot,' said Simon. 'But if Hollywood wants to go under, drowning in Michael Cimino's torrential wet dream may be as good a way as any.' Rourke, being the supernaturally loyal friend he has proven himself to be time and time again, reacted to the sniping by saying, 'If you put a piece of paper in front of me right now that said I could only work exclusively for Michael Cimino for the next ten years, I would sign it.' This kind of loyalty had previously been shown to Stuart Rosenberg, and would later apply to Francis Ford Coppola and Tony Scott too.

All in all, *Year of the Dragon* is a very good cop film, that suffers a bit from the preachy histrionics that Oliver Stone later became famous for in the films he directed himself. The story is interesting, entertainingly told, and at various moments quite thrilling and touching. Rourke's performance is solid in all aspects, but his changing hair colour (what Pauline Kael referred to as 'mood hair') does provide a visual distraction that diminishes its full impact.

As was the case with *The Pope of Greenwich Village*, it's hard to explain why audiences decided to stay away in droves. Was it because an action/cop film had tried to show an intellectual side as well? Or maybe because the female lead was so badly miscast, another ex-model with no acting chops and no chemistry with Rourke? (Possibly because of the anticipated firestorm over the racism charges, the main female character was changed from a tall, blonde, whitebread New York newswoman in Daley's book to an Asian American played by a former model named Arianne.) For whatever reasons, the film failed miserably at the box office. But this would not be the last time Rourke, Cimino and Dino De Laurentiis would work together.

During this time, Rourke gave a lengthy interview to *Playboy*. Some of the sentiments expressed indicate that the roots of his self-engineered downfall were already in place. The interview was conducted by Jerry Stahl, who would go on to write a fascinating memoir of his troubled life as a drug addict in Los Angeles, called *Permanent Midnight*. Rourke, who, going by his official birth date, was 31 at the time of the interview, was one of the hottest actors in Hollywood, his name on the lips of every studio boss, big agent and A-list director. For in the movie world, things move in a slightly different space-time continuum. Although Rourke had been seen in only a few films, none of which could be termed commercial smashes, behind the scenes his agent was setting him up in big movies for big money, based on his developing mystique. For Mickey Rourke was being described in mythical, albeit simplistic, terms as 'the new Brando, the new Dean'. But he proceeded to rag on Hollywood at every turn throughout the interview, so much so that Stahl called him on it. 'For a guy who makes a million dollars a picture you have a lot of contempt for the movie business,' stated Stahl.

'Definitely,' said Rourke. 'And I think to be part of this business, you have to be full of shit. That's why, at times, I think there is part of *me* that is full of shit because I am involved in this.' Stahl then continued to probe with this line of questioning by asking him how the insiders in the industry, those responsible for his million-dollar pay packets, might react to this point of view. 'You know, my agent says, "Mickey, you can't talk about the industry like that," and I say, "Hey man, *they* don't have to go to bed with *me* every night. When I fucking pull up the sheets and close my eyes, I gotta live with the decisions and the way I feel, and if I can't express that, then it's too fucking bad."'

But there was a contingent of people in the industry who still found that kind of attitude cool.

One such was Gene Kirkwood, one of the producers of *The Pope of Greenwich Village*. Kirkwood took a real liking to Rourke and wanted to make other films with him, putting a few projects into active development to show his sincerity.

Rourke was now so searing hot that it may actually have been the worst thing that could have happened to him, giving that artificial feeling of infallibility that leads many a promising actor to make ego-driven choices. He was choosing fantastic scripts, but all the projects seemed to fall apart for one reason or other.

For several years, there was a film biography of rock and roll legend Jerry Lee Lewis in various stages of development. Mickey Rourke was seen as the actor who could make the whole thing finally click into place, and he enthusiastically embraced the idea. There were a few drafts of a screenplay already floating around, but all involved agreed that a new draft should be commissioned to tailor it to the kind of energy and intensity Rourke could bring to the characterisation. He threw himself headlong into researching the role, studying every audio or visual recording of Lewis. He even learned to play the piano in the manner of Jerry Lee. But when the pages of the new draft started coming in they were very disappointing, sensationalist and superficial. Rourke was disheartened, and interest in the project started to sag once again.

The film was finally made a few years later, as *Great Balls of Fire*, with Dennis Quaid in the lead role. Quaid did an okay job, even though many thought his performance to be clownish and way over the top. But the film is light and airy and didn't make much of an impact at all. It can only be speculated as to how intense Rourke's version of Jerry Lee Lewis might have been. Quaid is a good actor, but he simply does not project the dangerous, barely contained passion of Mickey Rourke.

Kirkwood, Rourke and Rosenberg were also working together on some other interesting projects. The first of these was an intended re-pairing of Rourke and Eric Roberts, detailing the lives and deeds of Wyatt Earp and Doc Holliday respectively, with a grit and realism not often seen in traditional Hollywood Westerns. But once again, the initial heat sputtered and fizzled. Once again, the material would eventually make its way to the screen, this time in the form of two films released within a couple years of each other: *Tombstone*, with Kurt Russell as Earp and a dazzling Val Kilmer as Holliday, and Lawrence Kasdan's three-hour epic treatment of the same characters in his *Wyatt Earp*, starring Kevin Costner as Earp and Dennis Quaid as Holliday. Perhaps if Rourke had accepted the role Kasdan wanted him for in *The Big Chill*, the director might have cast his legendary Western figures differently.

The trio also tried to get another film biography off the ground – this time the subject was the legendary baseball icon Ty Cobb. Once again the project swelled with interest, before the wave dissipated back to nothing – only to return again a few years later, when writer/director Ron Shelton and actor Tommy Lee Jones teamed up to make *Cobb*, which earned Jones an Oscar nomination.

Kirkwood and Rourke refused to give up on the idea of working together. Their next project was based on William Kennedy's fantastic book on the life of Albany, NY-born gangster Jack 'Legs' Diamond, called *Legs*. Kennedy is a wonderful novelist, who also wrote, by conservative estimates, almost 50 drafts of the screenplay for Francis Ford Coppola's *The Cotton Club*. He also won a Pulitzer Prize for his novel *Ironweed*, which was turned into an interesting, if bleak, film with Jack Nicholson and Meryl Streep.

Rourke would have been perfectly cast as Legs Diamond, but the screenplays that Kennedy wrote inspired little interest from the studios. I interviewed William Kennedy for television a few years ago, and asked him about the status of *Legs* as a film. 'I still think it would make a great film,' he said. 'And at the time I thought Mickey Rourke would have been fantastic in it, he really got the character because he himself shared some of the same characteristics that made Legs Diamond an interesting guy – they had the same kind of animal instincts and an intensity for living life in the moment with complete immediacy.'

Rather than just giving up on working together, Kirkwood decided to help Rourke flesh out an ambition he'd been dreaming of since becoming an actor – to write, direct, and star in a film about the hard luck life of a boxer. Rourke called his script *Homeboy*, and his boxer is very similar to a guy he grew up around in Miami named Johnny Walker, someone he strongly identified with at the time. During his early times of struggle, Rourke was forced to make the decision as to whether to simply allow himself to drift into a life of crime, as so many others were doing around him – like Johnny Walker did, when his boxing career did not take off as he imagined it would.

Gene Kirkwood believed in Rourke's talents and, by extension, that he was capable of delivering something special with *Homeboy*. While Rourke was shooting his next film, he would use his weekends to go off to New Jersey and shoot some preliminary footage that he hoped would make it into the eventual low-budget project. Kirkwood personally financed these pre-production shoots, and would be instrumental in its final realisation. But what was to come next was a film that would cause Rourke to question his part in the whole moviemaking process. It would also bring him the kind of attention and star power that most actors only dream about.

# Chapter Seven

# SUPERSTARDOM IN 9½ WEEKS

**'The perversion of deriving pleasure, especially sexual pleasure, from simultaneous sadism and masochism.' –**
*American Heritage Dictionary definition of sadomasochism*

Mickey Rourke was being offered big-ticket films that would establish A-list careers for those who said yes to them. He was sent the script for *Top Gun*, but responded that he just couldn't picture himself saying the lines as written. Tom Cruise was not so particular, and became one of the biggest stars in history because of it. He was also offered a million dollars plus to star in *Beverly Hills Cop* – originally written as a starring vehicle for Sylvester Stallone, who passed on the project once it was written and rewritten several times at his behest. Rourke turned down the Axel Foley role because he thought the screenplay inconsequential, and just couldn't imagine himself speaking the dialogue. The script would be re-tooled yet again, making the character African-American and allowing a young comic actor named Eddie Murphy to step in and turn it into a star vehicle for himself.

Then came along a script called *Nine and a Half Weeks*, and Rourke saw something in it that excited him. But, as he would ruefully tell *Playboy*, 'I took that script for the right reasons, but I wasn't in total control.'

Rourke embraced the project with total commitment, although his frustrations with the process of making it would gradually escalate. He spent a lot of time researching and considering his character, even buying $12,000 worth of wardrobe for the role. It ended up sitting in a closet unworn, because director Adrian Lyne decided the clothing was not in keeping with his vision of the character.

I once spoke to actor Malcolm McDowell about his career, and he surprised me by saying he had made more money from the controversial pseudo-porn epic *Caligula* than from anything else he has ever done. Even though the film is tawdry and explicit, and was much maligned, it earned its makers a fortune that Caligula himself might have envied. This is similar to Mickey Rourke's agreeing to be in *Nine and a Half Weeks*, which would play in the same theatre in Paris for two solid years. Sometimes a film of dubious reputation can be the biggest boon to an actor's career. Rourke would gain more notoriety and popularity from this film than anything else he would ever do, even though it's essentially weak and uneven.

When examined closely, it's not so much a film as a series of tiny little vignettes that feature the same characters against a music video-type background. It was based loosely on a novel of the same name from 1978, by someone calling herself Elizabeth McNeil – though it's stated on page one, 'there is no Elizabeth McNeil,' which calls into question whether this is merely a pseudonymous novel, or a personal memoir of sexual adventure. The latter may well be the case, as the woman behind the story is clearly not proud of what she allowed herself to be a part of. (The story in the book is a lot darker, and does truly depict an S&M relationship, rather than just hinting at it like the film does).

When the filmmakers translated the book into a film, much was altered or inverted. When we are introduced to the character of John in the book, he is wearing a frayed pink golf shirt, scuffed running shoes and faded, worn khaki pants. Elizabeth, on the other hand, is described in the book much in the way that John ended up in the movie – as a successful, sophisticated professional.

Many of the set pieces in the book are radically altered, like the pair of them meeting at the street bazaar in Greenwich Village and buying her a scarf – in the book the scarf is a ratty little thing with character that costs $4, in the film it is a 'French shawl' that costs $300. The gender reversal sequence in the Algonquin Hotel is altered just enough to make it basically meaningless – in the book, the experience culminates with John violently sodomising Elizabeth in the hotel room. But what is drastically lacking in the translation from page to screen is the real violence and degradation of their sadomasochistic relationship.

The relationship in the film, courtesy of a limp dick screenplay by soft-core pornographer Zalman King (with assists from Patricia Louisiana Knop, King's wife, and Sarah Kernochan, who won an Oscar for her documentary *Marjoe!*), has little to do with S&M. What made the story of Elizabeth compelling was that she was an educated and sophisticated woman, with no previous impulses toward that kind of sexual experimentation, who found herself willingly engaged in it without knowing quite how it happened. In the film, as portrayed by Kim Basinger, Elizabeth is a ditzy, dreamy, quiet person who doesn't project any kind of intellectual point of view or strength – so we never question how she could have been seduced into this situation. Rather, we ask, 'If this is so bad and so uncomfortable, then why doesn't she just leave him?' The fact that the woman in the book felt she didn't have the power to resist this man poses the intriguing central question – why? What is happening to her? And how will she pull herself out of this vortex, or indeed will she? In the film there really are no such questions asked, there is no depth to the story whatsoever.

For a lot of people, *Nine and a Half Weeks* has become a guilty pleasure they revisit often. While writing this chapter, I asked a few female friends who professed a love of the movie to tell me their favourite parts: the food orgy in the darkened kitchen ranked highest, with mine being the smoky sequence in the ever-so-chic boutique in which Elizabeth is trying on an outfit. As John is doling out hundred-dollar bill after hundred-dollar bill for the outfit, Elizabeth asks him, 'Aren't you going to ask me how I like this?' John smirks and says, 'No.'

When I related this to Mickey Rourke, he laughed. 'It wouldn't be your favourite scene if you had to be there fucking shooting it. Let me tell you, that shit they pumped into the air to create that blue haze was fucking hell to breathe and it did a number on our eyes too.' At one point during the shooting, Rourke was so ill from the adverse bronchial effects of the blue smoke that he could not get out of bed for a couple of days. Adrian Lyne thought he was just being difficult, until he himself had to go to the hospital with the same symptoms.

Another ill effect of *Nine and a Half Weeks* was that it snapped the last straw in Rourke's marriage to Debra Feuer. Debra was as tolerant as she could be in dealing with his newfound success, and the behaviour that went with it. But when she read the screenplay and the original book, she expressed her extreme displeasure at her husband's involvement in a project like that. Rourke prepared for his role seriously, spending four months getting inside John. Feuer saw it as four months of increased self-absorption and selfishness. Rourke was quick to admit at the time that, 'making that movie was not particularly sensitive to my wife's needs.' Feuer also takes responsibility for the failure of the marriage. 'He was not a great husband,' she later said. 'But I was far from being a great wife.' The shooting of *Nine and a Half Weeks* and its aftermath would cause an irreparable rift that the couple was never able to remedy.

Ultimately, what makes the film so deeply flawed is that each segment has a different look and feel, giving the whole thing a lack of consistency. Sometimes the images are grainy and hazy, sometimes they are sharp and well defined. But this problem is indicative of the film as a whole. If you commit yourself to making a film that features sleazy sexuality as its central theme, you'd better be prepared to take it all the way. That was how the film was sold to Rourke. But ultimately, in Hollywood, the path of least resistance (and maximum box-office potential) is always taken. They can't have it both ways, but they often try through deceptive advertising. It was billed as this dangerous, darkly erotic film, but was really nothing of the sort.

There are a few different versions of *Nine and a Half Weeks* out there – a so-called European Cut, that promises to be more erotic than the version released in North America, and a mysterious work print (a rough assembly of footage used as a first draft of the film for editing purposes) supposedly circulating in this age of downloadable Internet movies. The work print is said to be over three hours long, and those claiming to have seen this version say it contains some very erotic footage shot for, but never used in, the final version of the film.

Rourke addressed the speculation in an interview with *Playboy*. 'What happened was that nobody had a lot of belief in the movie. Everybody was kind of timid about what kind of movie it was . . . I wanted to go a lot further than the film did.'

And just how far was that? 'I wanted to go *all the way* with it. I wanted to show every emotion that was going on between me and Kim.' He went on to say, 'I think that [Adrian] Lyne was under strict orders to make the film more mainstream. Even though we clashed on that I still think it is an interesting film.'

The story is a simple one – a lonely woman, who probably doesn't even realise just how lonely she is, meets a suave, good looking guy in a casual everyday encounter. She falls for him in a way that is new for her, but she goes with it. He is manipulative, a control freak, but a good lover and an interesting companion who masks his selfishness quite easily. Their relationship turns sexual almost immediately, and then evolves quickly into a more dangerous relationship that does not have any boundaries she can recognise.

In the book, the pain and violence inherent in this strange, erotic relationship entail John chaining or handcuffing Elizabeth to the bathtub while she's bathing, giving her numerous beatings, and gaining sexual pleasure from her pain almost every time they are together. None of

*Mickey Rourke and Kim Basinger in a promo shot for* Nine and a Half Weeks *(1986) – the soft-focus/soft-centred S&M love story that made both of them into 80's superstars.*

this abjectly cruel behaviour is evident in the film, with the minor exception of a few brief hints. (Rourke gives Basinger a swat with a leather riding crop in front of the shocked elderly leather shop owners, but even that is a lukewarm interpretation. In the book, John raises Elizabeth's skirt and hits her so hard on her bare thigh that it raises an angry red welt instantly.) There is a scene showing Rourke blindfolding Basinger before a sexual encounter, but it plays out against such soft lighting, and is shot so gently and performed so sensually by Rourke, that there isn't a hint of anything even approaching S&M.

The relationship becomes problematic for Elizabeth when she starts feeling that, not only has she lost control, but she also no longer desires to be on the receiving end of his manipulation. She finally just withdraws from it, and John, who was casually enjoying the selfish pleasure of it all, only finds the true extent of his feelings for her after she walks out the door for the final time. The duration of the relationship was nine and a half weeks.

British helmer Adrian Lyne is a good director, who does not just jump into a project simply because Hollywood is beckoning. In his 26 years as a filmmaker, the former TV commercial director has made just nine features – but they also include *Flashdance*, *Fatal Attraction*, *Jacob's Ladder*, and the controversial remake of *Lolita*. When he took on the job of directing *Nine and a Half Weeks*, he stated his intent to make a film that would not be well received by everyone. He wanted it to be an intense experience for the audience, but he was making the film with money supplied by the upstart Producers Sales Organization and the perpetually troubled MGM. Both wanted a say in how the film was made, how it was marketed, and, ultimately, in the final cut.

Mickey Rourke and Kim Basinger proved to be a volatile pairing at times, though Rourke would be diplomatic and gentlemanly whenever speaking of his co-star. 'It was hard sometimes to get Kim to come out of her trailer to go to work,' he said. 'Kim's a very private person. I think her representatives wanted her to do this movie a lot more than she wanted to do it. It was not the easiest time for her, but she delivered.'

Basinger was not quite so respectful when speaking about her co-star, calling Rourke 'the human ash-tray'. Recurring rumours that the sex scenes in the film were the real thing were answered by Rourke. 'Hey, I kept my pants on the whole time. Watch it closely and you'll see. People tend to see what they want to see.' As for Ms Basinger, with a few obvious exceptions she used a body double for the nude scenes.

Many of the criticisms levelled at the movie, about its disjointed nature and the lack of any clear motivation for the characters, relate directly to how it was edited. Director Lyne, producer Zalman King and Producers Sales Organization boss Mark Damon must have known that an X-rating was in the offing if they made the film as planned. But the distributing studio, MGM, was not inclined to go along with that. An X-rating slapped on your film means that it will not be carried by certain large theatre chains, cannot be advertised in newspapers, and will not be carried by the bigger home video outlets. So this is where the fissure occurred. As explicit and as out-there as the makers wanted the film to be, contractually they had to deliver a film that would earn an R-rating.

Glimpses of additional footage can be seen on the theatrical trailer and the DVD version that might have served to clarify some of the narrative gaps in the finished film. One such scene takes place after their first date together, on the boat to New Jersey. Elizabeth asks John if they are playing a game. John responds that it is anything that they want it to be. This may have helped clarify the line at the end of the film, when she tells him they both knew it would all end the second that one of them said, 'Stop.' There is also a snippet in the trailer of an edited scene involving Elizabeth and her boss at the art gallery. He is imploring her to give herself a lot more credit and telling her what a great person she is, to which she responds with a self-conscious smile. It might have driven the point home that she was suffering from major self-esteem problems, and so was vulnerable to the silky-smooth attack of this suave guy. (In the book, Elizabeth talks about how she never thought of herself as lacking self-esteem or confidence, which was why what followed was such a shock to her system.)

When the film was finally released, PR flacks claimed it was 'the hottest film since *Last Tango in Paris*'. But it wouldn't take long for word of mouth to report there was nothing all that hot about the movie, although it was not without its high-profile supporters. In Roger Ebert's glowing review for the *Chicago Sun Times*, he wrote, 'Kim Basinger and Mickey Rourke develop an erotic tension in this movie that is convincing, complicated and sensual . . . . I came away surprised at just how thoughtful this movie is, how clearly it sees what happens between its characters.' But this kind of praise did little to draw people into the theatres.

In watching the film now, you can see just how choppy and fragmented it is. (Rourke maintains that he has never seen the entire film from start to finish.) But it's not without entertainment value, if you take it for exactly what it is rather than what it was aspiring to be. This is what audiences in Europe and Asia did, making the film a big hit in regions outside North America – where MGM had made the bewildering decision (one of many such before they were bought out by Sony) to hype the film to the high heavens, but then to release it to only 28 theatres on its opening weekend.

Because of the global attention, and his coolly underplayed performance, the film made Rourke an international star. It is far from his best work as an actor, but physically he was looking as good as he ever has. It remains one of the most rented movies in the history of home video, once again proving that the critical reaction to a film actually means very little. If it contains something that a mass audience will gravitate towards, then it will be a hit.

Mickey Rourke was riding very high now. He was getting lots of attention and publicity, and was mobbed at the Cannes Film Festival. So what would be the next logical step for a new star of his magnitude? A Japanese television commercial, of course. Many big stars who sneer at TV make an exception when it comes to commercials for the Asian market. Everyone from Woody Allen to Harrison Ford to Brad Pitt has appeared in commercials produced in Tokyo, for astronomical fees and the promise that they will only air in Asia. Rourke was offered $500,000 for a few days shooting in Japan as a pitchman for Suntori whiskey.

He would soon start using his high earnings to dabble in side businesses, like buying a local gym and investing in a café with his hairdresser and friend Giuseppe Franco. But this was not really an attempt to diversify so much as being a generous soft touch for any friend who needed help.

With the release of *Nine and a Half Weeks*, Mickey Rourke had hit his zenith in terms of popularity and bankability. The experience had cost him his first wife, and had altered his sense of equilibrium. But he would soldier on in the spirit of non-compromise and unorthodoxy, although his life was already starting to show signs of unravelling.

# Chapter Eight

# FALLEN ANGEL

**'Alas, how terrible is wisdom when
it brings no profit to the wise, Johnny?'
– Louis Cyphre (Robert De Niro), Angel Heart**

Mickey Rourke was once asked what made him decide to make one of his most popular films, *Angel Heart*. His honest response was, 'I was about to lose my big assed house in California and needed a big paycheck fast so I wouldn't lose my house.' While this is true in the literal sense, there were also several other factors that attracted him to making this neo-*noir* – not the least of which was the opportunity of working with one of his idols, Robert De Niro.

But it was a curious position Rourke found himself in, and it would continue throughout his career. He was making money hand over fist, but spending it as fast as it was coming in. He was also taking care of his brother, Joey, who was fighting a long and protracted battle with cancer, and was a soft touch for any friend in need of money or help.

*Angel Heart* was another of those Hollywood films with a long and complicated gestation period. On release it also met with some controversy, entailing a hasty edit to prevent a Mickey Rourke film from getting an X-rating. It blurred the view of the film for many who never saw beyond the controversy.

*Angel Heart* is a darkly eccentric horror-*noir* mystery film, with a solid, passionate performance by Rourke and stylish direction by British filmmaker Alan Parker. Its source was a book by award winning novelist William Hjortsberg (who also wrote the screenplay of the Ridley Scott/Tom Cruise film *Legend*) called *Falling Angel*. It tells the story of a Fifties-era private dick named Harold Angel, who drinks a bit too much, smokes a bit too much, and who works only enough to get by. One grey New York winter morning, he is hired by a shady uptown law firm to track down an ex-crooner named Johnny Favorite (real named Johnny Liebling), who had a few hit songs leading up to World War II, but was then injured in a bombing raid in North Africa while entertaining the troops. While in the hospital recovering, he vanished, never to be heard from again. The mysterious man who hires Angel, Louis Cyphre, claims that he helped Johnny at the start of his career and is therefore owed something. He charges Angel with the job of finding Johnny because he doesn't like 'messy accounts'. Harry Angel takes the case, and finds himself pulled toward a dark world of black magic and voodoo, and the bayous of Louisiana where he finds Johnny Favorite's daughter, a pretty mulatto girl named Epiphany Proudfoot. As the mystery deepens, and everyone that Angel interviews about Johnny Favorite turns up dead, he begins to sense that he is a lot more involved in these events than he could ever imagine. It is revealed to him that *he* is, in fact, Johnny Favorite, who has been living another man's life to escape the fate he committed himself to, when he sold his soul to the Devil in exchange for fame. And it was Lucifer himself (Louis Cyphre) who hired Harry in the first place, to tie up all the loose ends.

Originally, the film rights to the novel were owned by Robert Redford and his production company, Wildwood Enterprises, who were planning to produce the film as a starring vehicle for him. The rights reverted because he was involved in too many other things, not the least of which was the burgeoning Sundance Institute and film festival. Redford's *Angel Heart* would have been radically different, in that Redford is very image conscious and rarely seen with a hair out of place. He could never play Harry Angel as an outright slob. And this is partly what made Mickey Rourke's performance so effective: he chucked vanity out the window and played Angel as grungy, dirty, greasy, worn out, dishevelled and weary as he had ever appeared on screen thus far. (He would top this with his appearance in *Barfly*.).

As Rourke said once he'd thrown himself into the film with full vigour, 'The character of Harry Angel seems to be a regular guy, a regular knock around guy in Brooklyn. He likes the simple life, going for a beer, getting laid whenever he can. He minds his own business, not everyone else's. He just gets by. He works, he reads the comics, and he takes a walk. One thing though, he has a little problem with his memory.'

Alan Parker wanted to film the book as soon as he read it. He certainly had the credentials and the talent to pull it off. Parker first gained worldwide attention in 1978, when he made the violent but brilliant *Midnight Express* (which won its young screenwriter, Oliver Stone, his first Oscar), and would go on to make such films as *Pink Floyd's The Wall*, *Mississippi Burning*, *Evita* and *Angela's Ashes*, among others. Parker adapted the Hjortsberg novel into a screenplay himself, remaining fairly faithful to the book (although a lot of the action Parker shifted to New Orleans takes place in New York in the novel). The screenplay was immediately deemed hot in Hollywood, and the upstart mini-major Tri-Star Pictures signed up to distribute the film after the freewheeling Carolco Pictures agreed to finance it.

When the casting process began, every big star in Hollywood had a look at the script. Robert De Niro – who would ultimately play the pony-tailed, bearded Louis Cyphre – was hotly pursued to play Harry Angel, but insurmountable scheduling problems made it impossible for him to commit. (He did, however, express an interest in the Cyphre role as he thought it might be fun to play.) Al Pacino was then approached about the Harold Angel role. Pacino liked the script, but was still in a self-imposed exile from moviemaking after his rather disastrous turn in the big-budget costume epic *Revolution* a year before, and didn't feel the film was strong enough to end his semi-retirement. Jack Nicholson was next on the list, and he too found the writing interesting, although he thought it was a bit close to *Chinatown* in tone. But his problem was the opposite to Pacino's – Nicholson had just done *Heartburn*, *The Witches of Eastwick*, *Ironweed* and a cameo in *Broadcast News*, all virtually back to back, so he had no time to make *Angel Heart* even if he'd wanted to.

Someone suggested Mickey Rourke to Parker, who thought the idea was worth exploring but immediately had a wary feeling about Rourke's reputation. 'Where does this reputation come from?' asked Rourke at the time. 'What have I done to be called a bad boy? I have never beaten up a photographer or caused a scene on a plane or thrown a tantrum in a hotel . . . so where does it come from?' Parker had heard that Rourke was volatile and hard to work with, because of his insistence that everyone take the work as seriously as he does while on the set. (Off the set, however, whatever he does is his own business.) This was no problem with Parker, who had dealt with volatile actors before but wanted to make sure that, if Rourke agreed to do the film, he would commit himself to it fully.

Harold Angel takes a bus ride into the heart of the old segregationist South, in Angel Heart (1987). His journey will take him on a personal route to Hell.

Rourke was eager to do the film – in fact, he was willing to do any film that would keep his gears greased, and pay him enough to keep his mansion and his gold Rolls Royce. Rourke would also admit that he was at a low point in his life emotionally as well. But ultimately, all his passion in the film was fuelled by the fact that he desperately needed a job.

Parker arranged to meet Rourke in New York City. The idea was to meet at a hotel where both were comfortable, but they ended up just walking and talking, block after block, mile after mile.

Parker was completely upfront about the fact that Rourke was far from his first choice. But, as the shadows grew long and the distance they had walked increased, Rourke became more and more passionate about the project and his desire to be a part of it. He had a healthy respect for Parker and his work, wanted to work with him on this down and dirty little *film noir*, and the idea of De Niro – the actor Rourke most admired – playing the Louis Cyphre role made it even more attractive. (Marlon Brando had been offered the role, but, characteristically, said he would do it only if he was required on the set for no more than a couple of days and was paid millions of dollars for it.)

The more they discussed the project, the more Rourke found that he liked Parker. Without realising it, the pair had strolled for over 30 blocks. By the time they had made their way back to the hotel, Mickey Rourke was playing Harold Angel – Harry's Brooklyn accent filtering into his speech, his walk becoming a shuffle. He was already embodying the character.

'The first thing Alan Parker said to me was, "You're going to behave on my set,"' said Rourke. 'I really tried to do that but he caught me at a really bad time. Right away I started seeing the same old studio bullshit going on with this film and I started getting angry.'

Rumours emanated from the *Angel Heart* set of some rather odd behaviour, but it was flowing in the other direction. It seemed that Parker was being overly hard on Rourke because of his preceding reputation, asserting himself strongly to let everyone know that he was in control of the set. Parker loudly dressed him down and yelled at him in front of the crew, upsetting Rourke on a few occasions. It bothered him particularly when he saw that the same loud verbal browbeating was not being applied to other cast members he believed equally guilty of the same offences (slight lateness in reporting to the set, resistance to rehearsing).

The female leads in the film were interestingly cast. Charlotte Rampling, long thought of as a French actress even though she was actually born in London, played the mysterious Margaret Krusemark, an ex-flame of Johnny Favorite now based in New Orleans where she works as a psychic. (In 1974, Rampling became something of a sensation when she starred in the darkly erotic film *The Night Porter*.) When Rampling arrived to begin work on *Angel Heart* her hair was cut in a spiky crewcut, but by the time she arrived on the set she was wearing a perfect wig, a thin sundress, and looked every part a haunted young woman in the 1950s.

The more controversial female casting was that of the exotically beautiful young actress Lisa Bonet as Epiphany Proudfoot. Bonet was widely known as the character Denise Huxtable on highly rated TV sitcom *The Cosby Show*. Only nineteen years old when she agreed to be in *Angel Heart*, she seemed to have no qualms about a scene of slaughtering a chicken during a voodoo celebration and allowing its blood to flow down over her bare breasts, or a lengthy nude sex scene with Rourke that ends with the pair showered with blood seeping from the walls and the ceiling.

Lisa Bonet was still doing *The Cosby Show* when she landed the Epiphany Proudfoot role, and its star, Bill Cosby, her boss in a very real sense, vigorously objected to her appearing in the film. There was even a suggestion that Cosby had Bonet fired from the show after she ultimately ignored his advice (although that seems unlikely, given how it was Cosby who saw to it that Bonet quickly landed another TV series called *A Different World*).

Shooting of the film went relatively smoothly, considering it was shot on location in New York City and New Orleans and the exteriors had to be dressed to appear locked in the 1950s. Rourke gave one of his most fully realised performances, as the hardboiled detective who is not nearly as tough as he looks or sounds. He physically expresses all his character's fears and doubts, culminating in a climactic scene where he screams his lines so loudly that he literally lost his voice.

Rourke's scenes with De Niro are also a lot of fun to watch. De Niro had mastered the art of scene-stealing through underplaying, but Rourke didn't react by wildly overplaying his scenes with him (the way a number of other actors have done opposite De Niro), but simply by matching him step for step. This dancing around De Niro's methods caused a little strain in their on-set relationship. Rourke is such a great admirer of his that he would never openly criticise him, but he did once allude to the dynamics of their working relationship. 'I grew up playing sports and enjoying and even thriving on the competitive nature of sports and found that a healthy thing,' said Rourke. 'But some people find that kind of competition scary, especially if they aren't used to it.'

But even that didn't stop Rourke from expressing his respect for De Niro. 'When I was doing *Angel Heart* I was really a mess,' said Rourke. 'I knew my lines and I was prepared probably more than I ever had been before because of the fact that I was facing Robert De Niro. His level of concentration and attention can be very intimidating. I have so much respect for him. Listen, when you work with someone like De Niro you either step up to the plate or you get smoked. I stepped up to the plate.'

Rourke also has some choice acting scenes with an old jazz musician named Toots Sweet (real-life musician Brownie McGhee), who also dabbles in voodoo and the occult. He is introduced to Harry Angel as a journalist working on a piece about an old band that played in New York, featuring Johnny Favorite. When Toots starts to realise that Angel isn't who he says he is, things turn desperately violent.

There are two scenes in this film that encapsulate the kind of acting that makes it succeed. One comes at the beginning of the film, when Angel is introduced to Cyphre by his attorney, Herman Winesap (played with oily effectiveness by Dann Florek of *Law and Order*). In this scene Rourke establishes Angel as a guy who approaches life with a casual, take-it-as-it-comes attitude, no matter who he's dealing with.

Another example of Rourke's expertise in underplaying a scene comes when he breaks into the home of an opium addicted doctor (Michael Higgins), who cared for Johnny Favorite when he returned from the war in North Africa with a major head wound. Angel uses quiet menace to intimidate the doctor into telling him what he needs to know; when that is not forthcoming, the detective locks him in his room to allow the doctor a taste of the withdrawal symptoms that will hopefully loosen his memory. When Angel returns the doctor is dead, seemingly by his own hand.

But it wasn't until the film was finished that the fireworks really began. The catalyst for the firestorm was the nude sex scene between Rourke and Lisa Bonet. We have long since gotten over the implicit racism that made it risky to have a sex scene between a Caucasian actor and a black actor. But consider that the black actress was playing a girl of only seventeen years of age; then consider the violence and gore that are made a part of this prolonged sex scene; then throw in the fact that she is ultimately revealed as the daughter of the Caucasian she is having sex with . . . and you have yourself a good old American scandal.

When the film was screened for its MPAA (Motion Picture Association of America) rating, it was deemed that significant cuts needed to be made to the more explicit scenes or they would

*Rourke's controversial love scene with the young Lisa Bonet, in* Angel Heart. *Their interracial coupling aside, it combines blood, the occult, and, with hindsight, incest.*

have no choice but to slap the dreaded X-rating on the film. Word again began circulating that Bill Cosby had actively tried to block the film's distribution, as he thought the controversy of the sex scenes would have a harmful effect on the family-friendly image of his TV show.

Alan Parker agreed to trim the scene, as he was contractually obligated to Tri-Star to deliver a film that earned a rating no harsher than an R. But Parker was only willing to cut, single frame by single frame, the bare minimum of material to secure that more friendly rating. And, in an odd bit of silly bureaucratic irony, all the excised material was put back into the film for its European theatrical and North American home video releases.

At the time of the controversy, Rourke had already started working on *Barfly*. Parker respected him enough to want him involved in the editing or, at the very least, to contribute his opinion. So he would drop by the *Barfly* set, where he and Rourke would huddle together in the Fish (Rourke's silver trailer, named after the 'SilverFish' that served as Francis Coppola's on-set home, editing suite and screening room). Parker even enlisted his help in dealing with the ratings board, asking Rourke to accompany him to hearings to appeal the harsh rating.

Curiously, when the film aired on American television for the first time, the sex scenes were edited out but replaced by snippets of material not in any of the theatrical releases. Moments

of flashback show Johnny Favorite during the war, and other little moments add a certain linear clarity to scenes that were intentionally left a bit obscure. The often strict British censors
didn't seem to have any problems with the sex scenes at all, but demanded that a scene involving a cockfight be eliminated completely (that scene was cut from the North American release
as well). But when *Angel Heart* was shown on British TV, the offending cockfight scene was
right back in there.

Budgeted at around $17 million, the film would go on to easily make that back on its March
1987 North American theatrical release alone, and it has been a consistent performer on home
video ever since – with a special edition DVD being released in late 2004.

*Angel Heart* is a solid piece of *noir* filmmaking – there are a lot of films that assume the *film
noir* label, but for once the term is accurate. Reviews were mixed, but once again Rourke's acting was singled out for praise. But *Angel Heart* is unfairly remembered mostly for the controversy that the sex scenes stirred up.

Rourke was happy with the work that he did on this film, and enjoyed his time on the set with
De Niro. But the ratings fight and the politicking that surrounded it once again left him with a bad
taste in his mouth. And still, as far as the mechanics of the film business went, the worst was
yet to come.


While fending off disillusionment with the movie industry, Rourke still actively sought out projects
he thought would be worthwhile and interesting. One such would be shot on a relatively low
budget in England, well away from Hollywood, and told an interesting story. The film was called
*A Prayer for the Dying.*

In *A Prayer for the Dying* Rourke plays IRA terrorist Martin Fallon, who flees Northern Ire-
land and his former life after he is involved in a botched bombing intended to kill a truckload of
British soldiers, which ends up killing a busload of schoolchildren instead. Arriving in London,
Fallon comes under the protection of English gangsters who aided his escape, while his IRA
comrades are looking for him because they fear he will compromise their ongoing operations.
Fallon reluctantly accepts a murder-for-hire job from London gang boss Jack Meehan (Alan
Bates) for money and safe passage out of the United Kingdom. But the shooting is witnessed
by a Catholic priest. Fallon thinks fast, silently stealing into the church to privately confess the
murder to Father DaCosta (Bob Hoskins). From there the story gets very complicated. Meehan
wants Fallon to continue to work for him as a hired killer, but Fallon has had enough killing and
just wants to escape to a new life. Father DaCosta is being pressured by the police to give up
this violent criminal, and Fallon's IRA comrades (including a nice turn by Liam Neeson) are closing in on him, with orders to either bring him back to Belfast or kill him. In the middle of all this
violence and danger, Fallon has fallen for Father DaCosta's blind niece, who lives with him and
acts as his housekeeper.

The conclusion of the film is a confrontation between Fallon and absolutely everyone who is
after him. In an explosion of violence, he is able to settle all the scores and is set free to go and
live a different life, and to try to cope with the demons of his past.

*A Prayer for the Dying* is based on the 1975 novel of the same title by Jack Higgins. Higgins'
crime/spy/mystery novels are known for an economy and straightforwardness that makes them

friendly to cinematic adaptation. But his ability to bury his themes almost subliminally in the action of the story became the root cause of this film's problems. Although it was being made in Britain with a predominantly British cast and crew, the money was coming from Hollywood – almost old-time Hollywood, in fact, as second generation mogul Samuel Goldwyn Jr. had set up his own production company (the Samuel Goldwyn Company) to make small films that he hoped would have an impact.

This film dealt with deep themes and issues, but Goldwyn panicked and tried to change it to the standard commercial action movie that no one who signed on for it wanted to make. When Mickey Rourke was offered the film and agreed to meet with producer Peter Snell, he was interested because of his familial connection to Ireland. But even in these early discussions, Rourke expressed his opposition to the amount of violence and killings in the book. He believed that element could be almost completely eliminated from the film without compromising the overall impact of the story.

At the time, director Franc Roddam was connected to the film, and was writing a screenplay adaptation that stuck very closely to the book and included the body count that both Rourke and Snell had agreed was excessive. Then an Irish writer was brought in to take a stab at the screenplay, Edmund Ward, who had previously adapted Jack Higgins' novel *The Violent Enemy* for a film made in 1968.

This draft was more to the liking of Rourke and Snell, and even Roddam thought it was worth proceeding with. (Even though everyone suspected he would try to get more of his own screenplay on screen once the shooting started.) Rourke then threw himself headlong into his research. He liked the book's themes and the way his character faced his dilemmas. Rourke travelled to Northern Ireland and actually spent a lot of time with Irish Republican Army members, in order to get the information he needed straight from the source and hear their view of things, and to develop a workable Irish accent. 'I learned about the problems, how the Catholic minority's civil rights get stomped on like the blacks in America,' said Rourke at the time. 'Fathers and grandfathers are unable to get work because of their religion. I saw the graveyards that were filled with guys who were killed at eighteen or twenty. I saw that I had the opportunity to make a movie that could say something positive and explain why a guy would turn to the IRA in the first place.'

There was even a suggestion that Rourke had had an IRA insignia tattooed on his body, but it remained unverified. As he said at the time, 'People just like to write shit that sounds good, don't matter if it is true or not.' And, as he pointed out, 'My grandparents came from County Cork and I wasn't going to have some Hollywood asshole make another *Rambo* out of that issue.'

But the development of this film can only be described as rocky. Franc Roddam quickly fell into disfavour. Both Rourke and Snell liked him as a director, but were not crazy about the direction he was planning to take the film in. So Roddam exited the project, citing those age old creative differences.

Rourke was isolated from a lot of the early discord as he was so steeped in his preparation, but as soon as work began with the replacement director, Mike Hodges, there seemed to be a marked discrepancy between the film Hodges was hired to make and the film Rourke had agreed to make. Rourke was incensed when it appeared that the plan was to make a Hollywood-style shoot-'em-up right from the start, with the slight twist being that this was a crime drama about the IRA instead of the Italian Mafia or Colombian drug lords. He and Goldwyn locked horns right away. 'Had I known this was what he wanted to do with this film I would never have come near it,' said Rourke. 'This is a serious story and it deserves a lot more respect and intelligence than he is giving it.'

The film Hodges was making was diametrically opposed to the film Rourke had in mind. Rourke was disturbed by the fact that they had replaced the first director, Roddam, with a replacement who seemed to be attempting to make the film in the selfsame way. To Hodges' credit, he did actually shoot a longer, more serious film than the producers' final edit. But the version released into theatres was considered so bad even by the director that he fought hard to get his name taken off the film. Rourke was similarly inclined, and stated as much – but his protests were meaningless, as his contract placed his name above the title of the film regardless.

While Hodges' version of the film was closer to what Rourke thought he was signing on to than the direction that Franc Roddam would have taken it in, he still felt that the Brit wasn't the right guy for the project. Rourke was quick to point out that he thought Hodges was a very good director in his own right (he made the original *Get Carter*, the later remake of which would feature Rourke in a small role), but he was too interested in making an action film. Hodges was the first to admit he was more comfortable with the kinetic aspects of an action movie than with the expositional scenes, but he also admitted the film needed to lend equal weight to both.

But for Rourke, it was the meddling Sam Goldwyn Jr. who harpooned the project. It was Goldwyn's money, and his risk, so he had the producer's right to do whatever he felt best for the film – but in doing so, he betrayed almost everyone who had believed in the project. 'I took half my usual salary to do this picture,' said Rourke. 'And I had to wait five months worth of delays before it actually started. Both Bob Hoskins and Alan Bates signed on because they said they wanted to work with me.'

Rourke felt he had shown his sincerity and commitment to the movie, and it really burned him that it counted for nothing. Much of his 'bad boy' reputation in Hollywood had stemmed from his deeply felt insistence that people around him should live up to their commitments. When he felt that they weren't, he got angry and frustrated and would not hesitate to openly call an old Hollywood establishment guy like Goldwyn an asshole.

These problems came to a boil when Rourke felt betrayed by producer Peter Snell. All throughout the early development of the film, Snell had constantly reassured Rourke that the subject matter would be treated with due seriousness, even going so far as to promise, 'we will make the film any way you want to make it.' But it was also Snell who decided not to tell Rourke that Sam Goldwyn Jr. was involved in the project until he arrived for the first day of shooting, and that Goldwyn was selling off the distribution rights in foreign territories on the strength of Rourke's name. As Rourke said, 'If I'd known Goldwyn was in on it, I'd have protected myself in my contract.'

But his contract was not specific in giving him any creative control, and he was susceptible to all sorts of interference. Goldwyn would challenge Rourke on the authenticity of his accent, or say that it was too thick and hard to understand. He would chide the actor about his performance, saying that it was too 'sullen' and 'lethargic' for the kind of film that it was. Goldwyn also

*Rourke intended* A Prayer for the Dying *(1987) as a statement on the Irish Troubles. But it became a melo-drama in which his IRA man finds love with a blind girl (Sammi Davis).*

suggested that the script be rewritten on the fly to make it 'tougher' – which by implication meant that he wanted more action scenes and shoot-'em-ups.

Rourke took the interference very personally, and felt it to be a betrayal. When he would baulk and argue his own ideas, Goldwyn would remind him in no uncertain terms that they had a contract. Rourke fumed, 'Goldwyn threatened to sue me every fucking week because I wouldn't make a *Rambo* movie – he fucking knew that I wasn't Chuck Norris or Arnold Schwarzenegger, he kept telling me that he was "afraid of the direction I was heading in" – he would send some flunky over to change my lines, to tell me to drop the accent, to tell me to shoot more people.'

Rourke was also furious about the decision to cast young British actress Sammi Davis in the role of the blind niece of Father DaCosta. He had no problem at all with her acting ability, but he was concerned that she looked so young. *Very* young. He was initially fine with the love scenes in the movie, but felt it would feel very awkward if the scenes were played with an actress who looked like she was barely out of her pre-teens. 'Of course when I was sitting in a room with these pricks they all agreed with me left, right and centre, but when I left the room they turned around and did whatever they fucking wanted.'

Rourke may have radically overplayed his hand in this case, but he got so irate that he threatened to call a press conference. He was coming from the street perspective of striking back when you feel you are being disrespected. What he remained (perhaps wilfully) blind to is that this is exactly how the business works on a regular basis. Producers lie to distributors; directors lie to producers; producers lie to actors. It is all just one big swirling mass of bullshit, between people who only ever say things they think other people want to hear at a given moment.

I asked Rourke about the experience of making *A Prayer for the Dying*. 'That was really the perfect example of everything that I found bad about the system at the time,' he said, 'that film didn't turn out . . . sometimes that happens, but what the fucking shame was that this one *could* have turned out, *should* have turned out because all the commitment was there, the talent, everything – it was wrecked by a gutless, talentless fucking guy who could not leave well enough alone.'

At the time, Rourke was quite open about how ashamed he was of the finished film and his participation in it. 'I'm not through with the issue,' he claimed. 'I'll make another Irish movie. I'll get across the point that I want to make and I am already looking into the rights to the story of a certain person whose story could help me do that.' That certain person was Bobby Sands, the IRA man who died while leading a hunger strike in 1981, in the Maze Prison outside Belfast.

*A Prayer for the Dying* was shot in England from September through November of 1986, and released on 11 September 1987. The budget of the film was low for the time, but still respectable at $6 million. It would end up with a theatrical release gross of just under $1.5 million. It did not succeed as an action movie, but they had cut so much of the meat out of the original idea that it couldn't work as serious drama either. The film was critically murdered, as well as being virtually ignored by audiences. Many critics ragged on Rourke because of the Irish accent he assumed for the role. But it takes guts to play a character with an Irish accent opposite Liam Neeson, a genuine Irishman. And at least Rourke's accent is identifiably Irish, not varying from scene to scene in the way of a lot of American actors (see anything by Kevin Costner that involves any accent at all).

*A Prayer for the Dying* has a very uneven feel to it, which indicates clearly how no one could decide what kind of film they wanted to make. But there are some interesting elements that do have merit – Rourke's performance being one of them. Had it not got caught up in the Hollywood greed machine (the same way that another film about the IRA would a few years later, *The Devil's Own* with Brad Pitt and Harrison Ford) then it might have turned out as a serious British crime drama, like *The Long Good Friday*. But what we are left with is an empty shell of a movie.

Bob Hoskins was actually terrific in the film, as a priest torn between doing what is right according to his faith and doing what is right as a man. I asked the jovial, talkative Hoskins about it during one of his visits to the Toronto International Film Festival. 'I had high hopes for that movie,' he said. 'But there were just too many cooks in the kitchen . . . too many people had decided that they knew what the movie needed to succeed when really, no one ever knows for sure. You have to be honest about what you are trying to achieve with a movie and if you are, the audience sees that.' And on working with Mickey Rourke? 'I liked Mickey a lot. I really enjoyed acting with him because he is so intense and unpredictable that he challenges the other actor in the scene to stay with him. The results are often nothing like you planned them out to be.'

The experience of making *A Prayer for the Dying* had a deeper impact on Mickey Rourke than he thought. When he finished the film and left England for home, he found himself sliding into a terrible funk. He had trouble sleeping and found himself becoming a psychological mess, unable to concentrate on anything long enough to consider it, much less commit to it. He actually developed an anxiety about working, because the experience was so profoundly negative he simply could not envision putting himself in a position where it might happen again. So Rourke stayed home a lot, or hung out with his brother Joey and his assorted motorcycle enthusiast pals.

But while Mickey Rourke was languishing in a haze of self-doubt and anxiety, there was a filmmaker who had a project he was certain Rourke would be perfect for. The script was called *Barfly*, and it had been kicked around from actor to actor. When it finally landed with Rourke, he would grab the role by the throat and deliver a passionate, almost surreal performance as Henry Chinaski – a thinly disguised self-caricature by author/poet/drunkard Charles Bukowski.

The film is about a drunk who has pretty much wasted his life, but who does harbour some talent as a writer. He gets discovered as such, but can't find it within himself to make the most of the opportunity and goes right back to being a drunk again. There are some wonderfully rich and subtle subtexts and subplots involving the power of love, friendship and communal support, whether your little community happens to be among high society or in the gutter. It is based on the life and works of Bukowski, but told in a loose, fictionalised sense.

The ragged Bukowski was a chronicler of the lowlife of Los Angeles – not the glitzy Beverly Hills, but East Hollywood, a place where dreams had long since been given up, forgotten or trampled on. He was the author of many books, mostly novels and poetry (although he would publish his screenplay for *Barfly*, and a follow-up memoir called *Hollywood*, which made it clear how little time he had for the movie industry types). In Europe, Bukowski had long since been revered as a writer who tells stories about the American experience that are just as real and as valid as those of Hemingway, Faulkner or Fitzgerald. Bukowski exposed the darker side of the American dream in a very poetic way, with language and sentiments that were dark and hard-hitting, but also poignant.

From the script's conception through to the release of the film would take the better part of a decade. The idea originated with French director Barbet Schroeder, who was a passionate fan of Bukowski's work and equally fascinated by his life. He had already shot a lot of documentary footage of Bukowski for French TV years before, and secured the rights to make a film based loosely on the writer's life and experiences. He also wanted Bukowski to write the screenplay, telling his story in his own words. Schroeder was completely undeterred by Bukowski's reticence, working on his resolve until he finally relented and attempted to write his first ever screenplay. Bukowski's small press publisher would take it to print in 1979, a full decade ahead of the film actually being made.

A few years went by and Dennis Hopper came across the screenplay, immediately passing it on to his friend Sean Penn. Penn loved it and declared that he would be very interested in playing the Chinaski/Bukowski role, *for no fee at all*. But that generous offer would only stand if his friend Hopper directed the film. Bukowski liked Penn a lot, liked his pluck and his indifference to Hollywood. But he simply would not betray his friend Schroeder, who was the reason that he wrote the screenplay in the first place. This led to all kinds of animosity between all involved. Penn dropped out of the project immediately, which was a big disappointment to Bukowski, who didn't fully understand that betrayal and double-dealing are simply part of day-to-day existence in Hollywood.

Schroeder kept plugging away and, after years of disappointments and reversals, the project finally came together. At the time he became very interested in talking to Rourke about playing Chinaski, the actor was in England making *A Prayer for the Dying*. It was a tough sell, partly because of his fragile emotional state, but there were also some thematic reasons that made him want to distance himself from the project. 'At first glance I really didn't want to do this movie at all, I have had some guys in my family die of alcohol abuse in their thirties so I didn't really find this subject matter attractive at all,' said Rourke. 'And I didn't even know who the fuck Charles Bukowski was. Barbet was following me all over England and the early time in the development trying to get me to do it. He then sent me a selection of Bukowski's books and I found them quite interesting.'

When I asked Rourke about *Barfly*, he nodded thoughtfully. 'Yeah, that is an interesting movie, an interesting character, dark – but dark for a reason. A lot of movies are dark for no reason other than they think that makes them look tough, but this guy had a soul that was dark, and he had gotten used to that and made it work for him.'

At the time Rourke said of the project, 'When I first read the script, I thought it was a very dark piece. It wasn't until we started shooting that I saw the humour.'

Strangely, although Rourke would deliver a *tour de force* performance, he would also describe it as one of the lowest points in his career. 'When I did *Barfly* there was literally no other role that I could have mentally or physically done,' he said. 'I was shot. It was not from drugs or booze or anything like that, I was just mentally broke down in a way. I was terrified to go to work because I had developed this phobia where I couldn't get into a car, I could barely leave my house, barely leave the room. I was terrified, I didn't trust anyone or anything.'

As he said at the time, 'I committed to the film about five months before we started work on it, but I was so fucked up after doing *A Prayer for the Dying* that I wouldn't even talk to Schroeder about the character until about two days before we started shooting.' Once Rourke was on board, Schroeder started looking for somewhere to set the film up.

The major studios were all squeamish about the subject matter, so he decided not to waste too much time even approaching them. Instead he looked to the so-called mini-majors and upstart production companies who were willing to take a chance on controversial material, just so they could profit from the added attention. One such, the Cannon Group, was run by a couple of high-flying Israeli film distributors who had decided to roll the dice as producers in Hollywood. Menahem Golan and Yoram Globus had made some interesting little films (*Runaway Train*, *Street Smart*, *52 Pick Up*) and some utterly ridiculous films (Bo Derek's *Bolero* and the record-setting arm-wrestling epic *Over the Top*, for which Sylvester Stallone was paid a whopping $12 million, almost twice the going rate for the biggest star salaries in Hollywood). The Cannon Group also had a lucrative distribution deal with Warner Bros. So when Schroeder brought them a film with Mickey Rourke attached as the star, they jumped on it 'in five minutes', according to the director.

At this time Rourke was already a huge star in Europe, so the thinking was that the project's

*Rourke incarnated Henry Chinaski, a self-portrait by drunken poet Charles Bukowski, in* Barfly *(1987). Taking a drink with him is Wanda (Faye Dunaway), his 'guardian angel'.*

earning potential in Europe and several other overseas markets made the relatively small budget a safe bet. But Rourke was monumentally uneasy about it. He had had a few bad experiences already, with his name used to pre-sell a movie in exchange for a larger role in its development – only to see that promise reneged upon almost instantly, once financing was locked into place.

Then it was disclosed that the Cannon Group was facing bankruptcy (it would actually go under about a year after the film was made) and the plug was almost pulled just days before principal photography began. Producer Fred Fuchs then made a desperate plea to his friend and frequent collaborator, Francis Ford Coppola, who stepped in and helped secure the project.

Shooting began, progressing as well as could be expected for a film that combined Charles Bukowski, Mickey Rourke and Faye Dunaway. Which might just translate as 'utter chaos' under any other circumstances. 'The set was anarchy,' said Rourke. 'Faye Dunaway was on the phone every day with her shrink for a couple of hours before coming out to work . . . I didn't know much about shrinks then, had I known more about them I probably would have been on the phone with one too.'

Bukowski was having a lot of fun on the set. 'I'd walk onto the set at 7:00 a.m. and there would be Bukowski and my brother Joe drinking beers. I would head over for my protein shake and get my vitamins and my ginseng and Bukowski would growl, "Hey, have a beer," and I would say, "I don't want a fucking beer – look at you two idiots drinking beers at seven in the fucking morning."

But Bukowski was cool that way – he would also say, "It's just a fucking movie, big fucking deal."'

Rourke sunk himself into the role of Chinaski, basing his performance in part on Bukowski himself. 'I met him, we talked a lot, he was an okay guy for a drunk,' said Rourke. He got along fine with co-star Dunaway, who was very impressed with his instincts and his willingness to throw vanity out the window in the interests of an effective performance.

When Bukowski came to the set after filming began, Rourke would immediately invite him into his trailer and offer him a long drink. 'He's a decent guy,' said Bukowski of Rourke. 'I liked him right away and when I saw him working on the film for the first time I immediately relaxed and knew that it would turn out okay.' Bukowski also broadly approved of his portrayal, with one minor exception – his choice of wardrobe. 'Rourke did a great job,' he said. 'But I didn't like how he wore dirty clothes all the time, ripped dirty t-shirts and baggy stained pants. No matter how fucking drunk I was when I got home I always washed my clothes and hung them out to dry so they would be clean the next day.'

The relationship between Rourke and Schroeder was a curious one, tinged by Rourke's recent experiences with directors who contrasted very negatively against his holy trinity of Coppola, Cimino and Rosenberg. 'Even though he was a prick and a baby,' said Rourke, 'he was really committed to the material and really knew what he wanted to get out of it.' Schroeder was not averse to playing people against one another to keep himself in the role of the good guy. He also threw little temper tantrums when he didn't get his way, which Rourke found embarrassing.

Rourke also struggled with his performance right up to the very moment the cameras began rolling. 'I was sitting in the make-up chair just before we started wondering what the fuck I was going to do with this piece,' he said. 'Then I heard Bukowski in the other room talking in that sing-song voice of his saying, "Hey baby, howya doin'?" – and I thought, "I'll do it like that, I'll just do it like that – I'll just add that voice and the rest of the stuff will fall into place."'

It certainly did. Rourke's performance is a marvel of nuance and subtlety mixed with the best kind of method acting. The affected voice works fantastically well, as it gives Henry Chinaski a kind of vaudevillian feel, as if even he knows that his whole life is actually one long, drawn-out performance. The direction is precise and to the point, there is no sense of over-stylisation or of the camera intruding. (There is also no composed score for the film, as associate producer Jack Baran selected the contemporary music while Rourke selected the few classical pieces that are heard.)

*Barfly* debuted at the 1987 Cannes Film Festival, where it was nominated for the Golden Palm and played to wildly enthusiastic audiences. The performances of Mickey Rourke, as the drunk with the soul of a poet, and Faye Dunaway, as his guardian angel Wanda, came in for high praise. Dunaway was nominated for a Golden Globe Award for her performance, while both Rourke and director of photography Robbie Muller were nominated for Independent Spirit awards (a hip anti-Academy Awards ceremony held each year before the Oscars, on the beach in Santa Monica). The film opened on 18 October 1987, and its opening weekend gross was registered at $45,900 – which seems scant, until you consider that it was only released on two screens. The final theatrical gross in North America was just under $4 million, with Europe reeling in another $7 million.

While the experience of *Barfly* didn't completely unload all of Rourke's negative baggage, it certainly helped alleviate some of its less tolerable aspects. One other glimmer of hope came in the form of one of the only real dreams he had had in the movie world, of getting his pet project *Homeboy* made.

Rourke was starting to believe that his future was in the low-budget independent world, both as an actor and a filmmaker. *Homeboy* was a script that he had written himself, that he also intended to direct and star in, about a boxer who leads a nowhere life, who is shy and awkward, but feels alive and vital when he gets in the ring. The character is named Johnny Walker, after a real boxer Rourke knew in Miami. Walker was so singularly devoted to boxing that he failed to develop any other part of his being; so when his career as a prize fighter did not pan out, it left him with no perceived alternative but to turn to a life of crime.

*Rourke as hapless boxer Johnny Walker in* Homeboy (1988). *The sympathetic woman in his life was played by Debra Feuer, whose marriage to Rourke was nearing its end.*

The casting of the film was first rate across the board, with serious actors like Christopher Walken, Kevin Conway and Jon Polito co-starring alongside Rourke. The film has the gritty look of guerrilla-style filmmaking, but the writing takes it up a few notches above that. This is a well-made film that has a considered feel to it, thought out well before it was ever shot, which is not something that can be said for a lot of indie films.

*Homeboy* actually did end up with a theatrical release in Europe, with the French being the first to see it in August of 1988. Finland, Sweden and Germany would follow with big screen releases in early 1989. There was no North American release until it arrived on video well over a year later.

But for Mickey Rourke, getting this film made was meaningful in that he had completed something that was simmering and brewing for a long time. But from here things would change for Rourke – in directions even he could not even imagine at the time.

But it was a wise move by Rourke not to direct the movie. He was not in the best frame of mind, and didn't think he'd yet learned enough about filmmaking from a technical standpoint. The last thing he wanted to do was blow it because of an ego-based decision.

Rourke asked New Zealand-born cinematographer Michael Seresin if he would like to make his directorial debut with the film. Seresin has been a favourite cinematographer of director Alan Parker throughout his career, and Rourke first met him when he shot *Angel Heart*. To date, *Homeboy* is the only film that Seresin has directed, but he remains one of the most sought after cinematographers around (having shot *Harry Potter and the Prisoner of Azkaban*, to name but one). Seresin certainly applied his talents to *Homeboy*, as the look of the film is one of its strong points. It lends power and strength to a harsh story about what happens to a person when he just isn't equipped to meet the real world head on, the archetypal story of a little guy eaten alive by the big, uncaring world around him.

Rourke's performance in the film is heartfelt and very poignant. There are some nice little moments where Johnny Walker's lack of wit and intelligence are heartbreaking. In one such, Kevin Conway plays a thug called Grazziano, who gives Walker some work from time to time. He offers Johnny an apple from a bag. 'Would you like an apple, John, they're Granny Smith's?' Rourke looks at him quizzically, then, with a slight touch of self-consciousness asks, 'What's Granny Smith's?' Conway then looks at him with sympathy and says, 'They're *green* apples, John.' Rourke plays Johnny as a beaten man who just hasn't realised he is beaten yet, failing to engage with the world on any level.

The fact that *Homeboy* got made at all makes it a triumph. This was a dream project that Rourke carried around for years, a story that he wanted to tell, that he needed to tell. His friend Christopher Walken and his wife Debra Feuer – who plays the sympathetic woman in Johnny's life – backed him all the way, helping to get the movie made in a manner that disgraced none of them. For Rourke was interested in telling a story that meant something to him, rather than just taking a big payday and walking through the job with no emotional connection to the material. Getting *Homeboy* made proved that Mickey Rourke has the kind of artist's tenacity that is rare in Hollywood, where the path most often taken is that of least resistance.

Rourke had found that low-budget indie films had their pluses and minuses. The positive side lay in the range of material one was exposed to, the lack of interference by studios, and the fact that all those involved in the project were generally on the same creative wavelength. The down-side was that the projects were risky and didn't pay all that well. They certainly didn't correspond with his now rather lavish lifestyle of fancy hotels and entourages.

But Rourke was still drawn towards projects that inspired and moved him. One such intrigu-ing, even bewildering offer came his way in Europe. *Francesco* came to Rourke at a time when

*Rourke and Helena Bonham Carter as Francis and Clare of Assisi in* Francesco *(1989). Rourke's Catholic upbringing made him an inspired if unlikely saint.*

it was getting harder and harder to justify remaining involved in the film business. He was still being offered studio work, but he was wary and weary. Then in Capri, Italy, controversial film-maker Liliana Cavani – who had directed the risque *The Night Porter*, starring Charlotte Rampling – approached Rourke about playing Saint Francis of Assisi in a film. Cavani had made a film about Saint Francis twenty years earlier, but had always harboured the desire to return to the subject matter, for the purpose of deepening her exploration of his life. But now, many people were asking why she would even consider an actor like Mickey Rourke for a project like this.

Saint Francis was born into wealth. He was a good looking man who was liked and admired by everyone. Once grown to a feckless youth, he spent his family fortune on self-indulgent pursuits like hosting large dinner parties for other idle noblemen. Then one day, while dining in an outdoor restaurant, he was approached by a beggar. He gave the man all the money he had with him, and his friends all mocked him for doing so. It got Francis thinking a lot more about the plight of the poor, and something changed in him. He found himself devoting more and more of his time – not to mention considerable sums of his family's money – on his new cause. His father thought it a complete waste of time and resources, and sharply rebuked him.

After being felled with a mysterious illness that nearly killed him, Francis became convinced that God had spared his life for one singular purpose – to continue the work he had started in the service of the poor. The rest of his life was spent selflessly reaching out to those a lot less fortunate than he was. Saint Francis of Assisi created the order of priests known as the Franciscans, and died at the young age of 46.

When it was made public that Cavani was seeking to cast Rourke in the title role, it seemed to some that she was betraying everything she stood for as a filmmaker. It seemed, on the surface, that Rourke was completely wrong for the role, and accusations of selling out were made against her. Many thought that she had cast an American star (British actress Helena Bonham Carter was also in the movie, but was a lot less known at the time) in the hope that his name would attract overseas buyers. Cavani defended her choice vigorously, saying that Mickey Rourke was the only actor she could think of who possessed both the intensity and the sensitivity to capture the Saint Francis she wanted to portray on film. The way she fought for her choice of Rourke inspired him to commit to the role, to live up to the faith she was showing in him. And beyond that, he was simply intrigued by the character from a historical point of view, having been raised as a Catholic himself.

Cavani's screenplay for *Francesco* was based on a novel by the legendary writer Hermann Hesse (author of *Siddhartha*), about the spiritual growth of the pious man who went from being a playboy to creating the Franciscan Order. Rourke read everything he could about Saint Francis of Assisi, and it may have been this that made him so effective in the low-budget film. One major weakness, however, is that he looks like the Mickey Rourke we were used to seeing. There was not even any real attempt to change his hairstyle, and while the film itself is quite engrossing and visually engaging at times, his oddly contemporary look tends to be a bit distracting.

The producer of *Francesco* was Roberta Cadringer, who is known for her Italian television epics on the lives of Jesus and Esther, and for a contemporary adaptation of *Dracula*. So *Francesco* does have that same epic feel, even though it's not achieved at the expense of the characters or the story. The musical score by the prolific composer Vangelis is both thoughtful and lush. But even though the drive behind the film is admirable, and the performance by Rourke – as the tortured soul who remains stoic and committed no matter what trials and tribulations come his way – is compelling, it doesn't really work in the way that all involved hoped that it would.

Rourke did not go into *Francesco* with any real hope of it being a commercial smash hit. When I asked him about the film, he said, 'Liliani Cavani made the whole thing worthwhile, that experience made me a better actor.'

Mickey Rourke's next film would be one of the more underrated offerings of the Eighties. It's an era that will never be written about as a golden epoch, but many of the films that came and went in a blink are looked upon now as minor gems. *Johnny Handsome* belongs in, or near, the top of that category.

I first saw *Johnny Handsome* on 12 September 1989, at its first press screening at the Toronto International Film Festival. The film was mesmerising but hard to categorise. It aimed high, trying to be an action film, a *noir* thriller, socially conscious and a quirky love story all at the same time. For the most part it did so without a hint of cynicism or self-consciousness, and nailed all of its objectives.

Based on the riveting crime novel *The Three Worlds of Johnny Handsome* by John Godey, the film concerns a smalltime career criminal named John Sedley (Rourke), who is called 'Johnny Handsome' on the street because his face is severely disfigured due to his mother's drug addiction while pregnant. Johnny is asked by his only friend Mikey (Scott Wilson) to help in the robbery of a rare coin dealership in New Orleans. Mickey and Johnny are partnering with a pair of slimy criminals, Rafe and Sunny (Lance Henriksen and Ellen Barkin) who betray them, kill Mikey and leave Johnny to be arrested and imprisoned. Rafe and Sunny use the money from the robbery to buy into a bar that used to be owned by Mikey, and arrange for Johnny to be killed in prison. But the assassination is botched, leaving Johnny in the prison hospital where he meets a bighearted doctor (Forest Whitaker) who tells Johnny there might be a way out for him.

*Before: Rourke as Johnny Handsome (1989), a criminal whose facial deformity destroys his self-esteem. It was the first time he played a role under heavy prosthetic makeup.*

Dr. Resher believes that, if he can surgically repair Johnny's face and give him a new identity, then the self-esteem and self-respect he develops may preclude any further criminal recidivism. Johnny agrees reluctantly to participate in the programme because he wants to gain a new identity out of the deal. The Cyclops in this odyssey comes in the form of a New Orleans detective, A. Z. Drones (Morgan Freeman). Drones believes that Johnny is a criminal by nature, and that nothing that is done to his exterior will change this. But the surgery goes ahead as planned, and is a success. Johnny Handsome is turned into a cool looking guy (i.e. Mickey Rourke).

With his new identity, Johnny is given a work release programme at the prison hospital and

*After: Johnny Handsome emerges from plastic surgery to discover he looks like Mickey Rourke – seen here with the duplicitous Sunny (Ellen Barkin).*

gets a job at a local shipyard. He hatches an idea to avenge the death of Mikey by approaching Rafe and Sunny with another robbery plan, to rob the shipyard during the day when all the cash comes into the ATM machines around the area. But what Johnny doesn't anticipate is falling for a girl who works as a secretary at the yard. Donna (Elizabeth McGovern) falls heavily for him too, and is drawn into the violence because of it. The robbery takes place, and so does the intended double-cross of Rafe and Sunny. But Drones has been into them all along, because he has been watching Johnny. Before he can act, Sunny finds out that the newly minted John Mitchell is actually Johnny Handsome. She kidnaps Donna, to ensure that she and Rafe get the money from the shipyard heist, and at the same time eliminate Johnny Handsome. The meet to swap the money for Donna is scheduled for a cemetery late at night. As the gunfire explodes, Rafe, Sunny and Johnny are all killed. Drones appears after the shoot-out to console the hysterical Donna. Looking down at her dying boyfriend, he says, 'You didn't tell her about this part, did you Johnny?'

The film opens with the haunting slide guitar strains of composer Ry Cooder, and slides into the dark, misshapen face of Mickey Rourke, laden with prosthetic makeup, strolling down a rainy French Quarter street in slow motion. The momentum that gathers with every sequence is all to the credit of director Walter Hill. Hill began his career as a screenwriter and was clearly influenced by Sam Peckinpah. In the Seventies he wrote the screenplays of such hardboiled crime films as *Hickey and Boggs*, with Bill Cosby and Robert Culp, did a fantastic job of adapting Jim Thompson's novel *The Getaway* for Steve McQueen and director Peckinpah, and had a hand in the creation of the original *Alien*. As a director he has made some interesting and underrated films like *The Driver*, with Ryan O'Neal, and *The Long Riders*, a very Peckinpah-esque revisionist western.

Rourke was not the first choice to play Johnny Handsome. Al Pacino and Hill had already worked closely together on the project, to develop the screenplay. After many revisions, Pacino had decided that the film would never rise above the status of a B-movie potboiler. Rourke stepped in because it gave him the opportunity to work on another big budgeted studio film, with the corresponding pay cheque attached. But, once committed, he embraced the physical and acting challenges that the role presented. He had to create a character who spoke with a very distinct and affected voice because of his facial abnormalities, and also to take on a secondary adopted personality. In the process, he delivered one of his best screen performances he has given, relying on underplaying his scenes rather than all the histrionics that many film actors fall back on. His Johnny Handsome is played as a perfect criminal who lives by a certain code of behaviour. If that code is violated, then he has no choice but to exact revenge. Rourke also plays the surgically corrected John Mitchell personality with such a cool attitude that you can see this is the man that Johnny Handsome always fantasised he could be.

This was also an early example of just what a powerful performer Morgan Freeman is. He plays Drones as a tough, cynical, but very practical cop. In a lot of Hollywood offerings, the tough cop would have melted in the face of sadness and decided to help this poor criminal with his new life. But Freeman plays his character as a guy who has been around too many criminals to be fooled by temporary respites in their behaviour. As he tells Johnny early in the process, 'I know what you are on the inside,' which is one of the most telling lines in the film. When I spoke to Freeman in New York, just after he made *Se7en*, I asked him about the experience of working with Mickey Rourke. He smiled and said, 'I had a good time working with Mickey – he is a very authentic actor.'

And the film has a similarly authentic look and feel to it, shot entirely on location in Louisiana, everywhere from the old quarter of New Orleans to the Louisiana State Penitentiary in Angola and the Avondal Shipyards.

When I asked Rourke about *Johnny Handsome*, he shook his head slightly and nodded. 'He [Walter Hill] was trying to make about three different movies within the one movie,' said Rourke. 'And I think because of that all the elements in the film suffered, because they no longer had the authoritative weight of being followed through on.'

*Johnny Handsome* did not fare well at the box office, earning less than $10 million, and has been released on DVD only in a 'pan and scan' version. When Mickey Rourke made the film he was still a big star, his name appeared above the title and he could command seven-figure salaries. But things were changing in his life, and he was losing his battles with his personal demons. He was looking for something or someone to fill a big void, and on his next film he would find it. It crept up on him from behind, and from thereon his life and career would rapidly unravel.

# Chapter Nine

**'There is always some madness in love. But there is also always some reason in the madness.'**
**– Friedrich Nietzsche**

When Mickey Rourke's marriage to Debra Feuer officially ended in 1989, the outcome was amicable and reasonable. 'I was ready to simply settle for half of the stuff that we gathered together during our marriage,' said Feuer. 'But Mickey, being Mickey, gave me everything, house, car, lots of money, far more than I was expecting. His lawyers were beside themselves trying to talk him out of doing that but he said he wanted to take care of me then because he felt he had let me down throughout our marriage, something I never agreed with. We love each other and share a bond, we just couldn't live together as man and wife.'

When Rourke moved on from his first failed marriage, he did so with no negative baggage. 'Throughout our marriage Mickey and I would have some big blow ups,' admitted Feuer, 'we are both passionate, fiery people. But he never, ever laid a finger on me in anger, ever. Not only that, but I never ever feared that he would, that just isn't part of his make-up.' But by the time that his second marriage, to model/actress Carre Otis, hit its full stride, the couple's relationship was always written about in the tabloids prefixed by words like 'turbulent', 'troubled' or 'volatile'.

A lot has been written about the relationship of Rourke and Otis, most of it just invention and salacious gossip. Their marriage has been dismissed as one of those Hollywood romances that explode into immature petulance and violence, due to ego and lack of self-discipline. But again, this is based on invention with only the slightest hint of distorted fact.

The truth of the matter is that his relationship with Carre was deeply important to Rourke. As he told me, 'I will never get over her. She will always be a part of me.'

Their story starts with the film *Wild Orchid*, which was seen as a kind of follow-up to or extension of the erotic exploration of *Nine and a Half Weeks*. *Wild Orchid* deals with a young woman's sexual awakening in a place both unfamiliar and exotic to her, the kind of theme often attempted, but rarely achieved with any effectiveness in a mainstream feature film. Rourke decided to roll the dice a second time with Zalman King, only this time King would not only write the screenplay but direct the film as well.

While the finished result is far from great, there is something about the film that qualifies it as a cultish guilty pleasure that can be fun to watch – not least for the well-staged erotic content, but also for the fantastic Brazilian scenery, music and energy. When held up alongside *Nine and a Half Weeks* in terms of erotic content, it's a considerably more arousing experience – though the former film did attempt to reach a place of greater emotional depth than *Wild Orchid*.

Zalman King is a curious character in Hollywood. He has virtually cornered the market in soft-core, rouge-hued, sex-soaked video features and made-for-cable TV series. Born in Trenton, New Jersey in 1941, King was at first a professional deep-sea diver in the 1960s, who then decided to give acting a try in the 1970s. He made his big screen debut in something called *The Ski Bum* in 1970, and would go on to appear in a number of exploitation films with titles like *Galaxy of Terror.* But King ultimately decided that the only way to find your opportunities in Hollywood is to create them yourself. 1980 saw the release of the first film that he wrote himself, called *Roadie.* After his experience co-writing and co-producing *Nine and a Half Weeks*, King decided it was time to direct a film himself. His first effort, made in 1988, was called *Wildfire.* He has not looked back since. His erotic (in a Harlequin Romance sense) series *Red Shoe Diaries* is constantly running on cable stations throughout the world, and King is married to Patricia Louisiana Knop, co-screenwriter of both *Nine and a Half Weeks* and *Wild Orchid.*

When Rourke signed on to make *Wild Orchid*, it was on the understanding that he would be involved in developing the screenplay, casting the major roles and designing the overall look of the film. Years previously, he'd believed he would be given similar artistic control over *Nine and a Half Weeks*, but without a contractual guarantee it became just another retrospective regret. This time, if he was going to go down that same dangerous cinematic road again, he needed to feel sure that he actually had some control. One thing that Rourke and King did agree on from the outset was that the climactic love scene between Rourke's character, a mysterious business tycoon, and a beautiful young international business attorney (eventually played by Carre Otis) would be the most erotic and passion-filled scene ever played out in a mainstream film.

The story is about a voluptuous but innocent young woman, who has trained in international law and accepts a job with a firm that sends her to Brazil. There she meets a senior partner who is doing some business with a suave, shady high roller who becomes infatuated with her. He quickly identifies her needs and takes her on a wild tour through a sexual fantasyland that culminates in a passionate explosion of lust.

To say that Carre Otis was not the first choice for the role is an understatement. Throughout the early development of the film, right up until the production team began to assemble in Brazil, she was not even on the radar screen. Initially Brooke Shields was eager to get involved, seeing it as a way of shedding the adolescent image that had persisted from the time of her performance in Louis Malle's risqué *Pretty Baby,* through the Calvin Klein jeans ads that made her a household name as a young woman. But there was an element that she could not reckon with – the nudity. She would agree to do the film, only on the condition that a body double be used for her during the sex scenes. But, given the way the film was being shot, it would not have been possible to use a double without it being clearly obvious and detracting from the audience's ability to connect with the character. So Shields parted company from Rourke and King.

Enter Cindy Crawford, one of the original 'supermodels'. Crawford was eager to make the leap to the big screen and seemed to really like the *Wild Orchid* screenplay – so much so that she actually went to Milan to be fitted for her costumes by designer Luciano Soprani, while the rest of the production staff headed to Brazil. But then, unexpectedly at the last minute, Crawford began making demands that all the sex scenes involving her character be written out of the script. King was incensed, as the film is entirely about her character's sexual awakening and her exposure to a wild, overheated sexuality.

While Cindy Crawford has clearly gone on to a wildly successful career in modelling and prod-uct endorsement, she never did make the leap to the big screen that she yearned for. (She did make a lame film called *Fair Game*, opposite William Baldwin, that bombed very quickly.) I had an unforeseen opportunity to speak to Ms Crawford, when we both sat in the same row on a flight from New York City to Toronto in January 2005, and asked if what I had read about the reasons for not making *Wild Orchid* was true. 'It wasn't quite that cut and dried,' she said. 'On paper the script was interesting and the sex scenes were written kind of simply and not very descriptively. The idea was clear for what the scene was going for, but it wasn't until later that I started to get the idea of how these scenes would actually look and what was expected of me in terms of my "per-formance" – I just decided that that really wasn't the best way for me to make a film debut.'

It left the production without an all-important leading lady, and with the wheels already turn-ing. Running out of time and with their options dwindling, King started seeing people in haste, including model Carre Otis, who had never stepped in front of a movie camera in her life. King quickly read her for the part. What she lacked in experience, she more than made up for in fit-ting the physical criteria of the role. Rourke had envisioned a tall, full-lipped, very sexy woman who was not fully aware of just how sexy she was. After Carre read with Mickey for the first time, he would tell King that he sensed she 'had something' and 'could be great' in the part. But King was a bit skittish, knowing that the success of the film hinged on getting the right woman for the role. He would audition Otis three more times before he finally started to see the qualities that Rourke seemed to pick up on instinctually, upon their first reading together.

Once the cast and crew were assembled in Brazil, there was a natural gravitational pull between Carre Otis, the neophyte, and co-star Jacqueline Bisset, the older, wiser woman who played her boss in the film. Bisset had been hotly pursued for the Elizabeth role in *Nine and a Half Weeks*, but turned it down because of the nudity and the darkness of the piece. Bisset had been there and done that many times over, and could warn Otis of the pitfalls that awaited a sexy young woman in the all-devouring movie business. Otis would credit Bisset with helping her gain the confidence to play her character and the sex scenes with a relaxed demeanour, allowing her to concentrate on what was being expressed in the scene rather than just what was being shown.

As the shoot progressed it also became obvious that Rourke and Otis were growing close offscreen as well. As Bisset confirmed, 'It was not a secret at all that they were together. But that, I think, had a positive effect on the film we were making.' Mickey and Carre began spend-ing more and more time together and Rourke became increasingly protective, showing an obvi-ous pride when Otis would nail a difficult scene.

The big climactic sex scene was scheduled to be the last sequence shot. King wanted all the momentum he had carefully orchestrated throughout the Brazilian shoot to explode all over this one scene. But one week beforehand, there was another sex scene planned involving Carre and Canadian actor Bruce Greenwood, in which Otis's character, at the behest of Rourke's charac-ter, has a sexual encounter with a stranger she meets at a masked ball. Otis was fine with the scene, she knew what was expected of her and she came to the set prepared. It was Rourke who was having problems. There were reports from the set that he was showing signs of obvi-ous jealousy, and was extraordinarily concerned about the shooting of the scene.

I asked Bruce Greenwood in Los Angeles about his recollection of the incident. He thought for a few moments, then said, 'Well, that scene, as is the case with all nude scenes and scenes that involve that degree of physical intimacy, they are difficult of course. But what I remember about that set was that it was closed and the director and the crew were always respectful and made

*Bike fan Mickey gives a ride to model Carre Otis in her first acting role,* Wild Orchid *(1990). This piece of soft-core erotica set the stage for the couple's tempestuous marriage.*

the difficult nature of the scene as easy for us as they could.'

I then asked about the rumours from the set that Rourke behaved jealously during the shooting of the scene. 'I heard something about that,' said Greenwood. 'But I don't remember it as being anything problematic. I remember that they [Rourke and Otis] were a real item at the time, so the fact that his girl was getting ready to do a nude sex scene with another man was probably a bit unsettling, I can't imagine how it would not be, but there was never a problem that I was made aware of.'

That scene was filmed without a hitch, and then came the big day. But it was Rourke who showed signs of anxiety and panic. While Otis was once again calmly prepared, it was reported that Rourke refused to come out of his trailer. He was complaining, allegedly, about his wardrobe – oddly enough, since it was a nude love scene. Then the word was that Rourke hated the dialogue, or hated his make-up. There were a few extra days built into the budget to cushion any reasonable eventuality, so the scene was simply scheduled to be shot the next day. There was a report in *Playboy* that said the crew had a name for the delays: 'Mickeyitis'. But others on the set said they had never heard that term and never found Rourke to be difficult to work with at all.

The *Playboy* report was part of a racy pictorial that showed several rather explicit photos of the sex scenes with Rourke and Otis (and the scene with Otis and Greenwood, as well as the sex scene between the maid and the stud against the warehouse wall). When that particular issue hit the newsstands, Rourke flipped his lid and immediately filed suit against the producers of the film for selling the photos to publish without their permission. Rourke would win an out-of-court settlement for an undisclosed amount.

The next day arrived, and this time both Mickey and Carre were late to arrive at the set. Rourke called in and said the reason for the delay was simply that he had overslept. After half the day went by, Otis and Rourke finally arrived on the set in their robes, after quietly preparing in his trailer. The set was closed, with only the most essential crew members allowed. Once the lighting was set and the scenes were blocked, the doors to the set were closed and a security guard placed outside the door as an added precaution. Rourke and Otis took their places and King quietly called for action. He was working on the correct assumption that, once they got going, the crew would be able to shoot the scene just once. To ensure its success, King covered the set with three cameras to cover all the angles at once, to cut down on the number of takes and set-ups – one covered the action from overhead, the other two covered from right to left and left to right. The scene quickly generated enough energy and heat to delight everyone involved. Both actors allowed the passion and the feelings that they had for each other to add to the erotic veracity of the scene. Whatever your feelings about *Wild Orchid*, this scene really is among the most erotic ever filmed for a mainstream movie. Just as Mickey Rourke and Zalman King had planned it to be.

Just before the release of the film, tabloids started to crackle with the rumour that Rourke and Otis, who were now publicly an item, had actually had sex during the sequence. And in a move that was pure PR, no one bothered to deny it outright. So, did they or didn't they? Maybe. And it's the *maybe* that makes the scene all the more erotic – though Rourke typically laughs off any suggestion that it was the real thing, and Carre Otis has denied it outright.

The film was released on 18 April 1990, and while the critics were brutal in their attacks, the box office takings were okay. It was not a major hit, but the domestic box office was over $15 million, with another $18 to $20 million from foreign territories. The film was also nominated for two of the infamous Razzie Awards – Mickey Rourke was nominated for Worst Actor and Carre Otis for Worst New Star.

The critics took a great deal of pleasure in dumping all over the film, and on Rourke in particular. He was written off as a sleazy, greasy looking character who cruised through his movies, as if they were mad at him for not living up to their idea of his former potential. But, while writing this chapter, I conducted a little field experiment. I went out looking for a replacement copy of *Wild Orchid* in downtown Toronto, a city that prides itself on being very film literate. I went to seventeen different stores and video outlets and found that not a single one had any copies left in stock. I also checked with a few secondhand DVD shops and the same was true there – one vendor even told me I was 'the third guy to ask for *Wild Orchid* in less than a week'. So there is something that the

*Mickey and Carre at L.A.'s Roxbury Club in 1990, before the rumours of drug addiction and violence. 'I will never get over her. She will always be a part of me,' admits Rourke.*

mass audience sees in this film that makes it worthwhile, whatever the critics say.

Carre Otis was born in San Francisco on 28 September, 1968. Her father is a corporate lawyer and her mother a fundraiser. She claims that both her parents were heavy drinkers, as she herself became by the ridiculously young age of eight. Carre ran away from home frequently as a kid and dropped out of school at fourteen. She decided to stop by modelling doyenne Eileen Ford's office on a roll of the dice, and it changed her life. Because of her five feet ten inch stature and willowy body, she was able to gain attention quickly.

By her late teens she had moved to Paris, where the hot young model worked for Donna Karan and Calvin Klein to the tune of between $15,000 and $20,000 per day, and was exposed to the darker side that the modelling industry is very good at keeping under wraps. Agents kept their young models fuelled with cocaine to keep their weight down and their energy up – something that Otis had to deal with constantly, as she had a tendency to pile on the pounds relatively easily.

Reportedly, Carre was filled with a kind of self-loathing during her modelling career. She enjoyed the attention, the money and the exotic lifestyle of a successful model, but she was also being sexually manipulated by older men connected (or claiming to be connected) to the modelling industry.

So Carre Otis was no wallflower when she signed on to make *Wild Orchid*, and met Mickey

**85**

Rourke. Once their relationship was established in the public eye, persistent gossip started circulating in the tabloids about Rourke having completely taken over her life and prohibiting her from working. One story that kept popping up was that Otis had to turn down an offer in excess of $1 million, for no other reason than Rourke refused to allow her to work in the modelling industry anymore. 'A lot of bad things were being said about Mickey,' acknowledged Otis. 'The talk was that Mickey didn't want me to work and that was true, but the decision not to work was ultimately mine and mine alone.' Otis was also one of the first supermodels to openly sport tattoos, including one of Mickey Rourke's name. (She would be quoted much later as insisting, 'Never ever get someone's name tattooed on you, never ever ever.')

Their relationship bore the added weight of media attention. Rourke told me that it never really bothered him, but there is evidence to the contrary. They would be hounded by the insidious paparazzi, who would cower hundreds of yards away, concealed by bushes or walls, so they could snap pictures of Rourke and Otis on vacation, or get a couple of shots of Carre on a horse, topless. Rourke and Otis certainly understood that this kind of attention is part of the life they have chosen, but the light focused upon them ultimately became too intense.

Mickey Rourke and Carre Otis were married on 26 June 1992 in Big Sur, California. Almost immediately, the entertainment press began reporting that violence and drug use were a regular part of their volatile married life. When asked about it, Carre guardedly answered, 'All I would say is that there was always a certain amount of aggression in our relationship.' But she was not saying which way that aggression was flowing.

Two years later, in mid-July of 1994, the police were called. Rourke was arrested, and charged with spousal abuse and assault. His mugshot and details of the charges went out on the wires, picked up by newspapers, magazines and TV shows the whole world over. The headlines were lurid, the details recounted in snide prose. A kind of I-told-you-so smugness permeated coverage of the arrest. The fact that the charges against Rourke were dropped almost as quickly as they were filed wasn't given quite the same prominence, if it made the papers at all.

Rourke and Otis were going through a very difficult time. The press were already hinting about her reputed problem with drugs, specifically an addiction to heroin. Carre herself was open about the fact that her drug problem stemmed directly from her problems with self esteem, yet still the press seemed determine to find a way to blame it on Rourke. There was constant chatter about Otis 'ballooning' to over 170lbs – whereas, in the real world, a woman of her height can carry 180lbs and look spectacular.

There was certainly truth in the rumours about heroin, as it was something Carre talked about publicly. And it was true that their relationship, as Mickey tried to get her off drugs by whatever means necessary, was spiralling into a maelstrom of barely contained rage and frustration. But the fact that he arranged to take her to a special clinic in Mexico, for treatment with a radical new drug that promised rapid withdrawal from dependency, went largely underreported. Carre had almost died from a heroin overdose, and her problems would certainly test his love for her – a test that he passed with flying colours.

# Chapter Ten

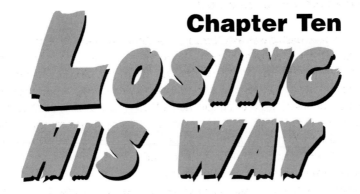
## LOSING HIS WAY

**'Be careful that victories do not carry with them the seeds of future defeat.' – *Sun Tzu***

Mickey Rourke was growing more and more disillusioned with what was happening in his life. His marriage to Carre Otis was wonderful and difficult in equal measures; his career was still yielding him big money, but it was going out as fast as it was coming in. His brother Joey was still fighting a valiant battle against cancer, his expenses met by Mickey.

And Rourke's reputation as a rebellious bad boy had taken a turn towards a darker, more alienating perception of him. Being a rebel is something that has a certain cache in Hollywood, but a reputation for being difficult, almost untouchable, is not something that many recover from. Ironically, however, a great deal of that reputation was almost unfathomable to Rourke himself, and to those around him. Debra Feuer will tell any interviewer who cares to ask that Rourke is simply nothing like the brawling hell-raiser of repute – in fact, in her experience he is the exact opposite.

Rourke despises the tough guy label because he has always felt that there is no such thing in Hollywood. As he told interviewer Jerry Stahl, 'There are a lot of guys who like to pretend. They are trying to project some kind of tough guy image, but anyone can see through it; if you want to be a bad dude, go to jail. Don't be bad in a Hollywood restaurant with a bunch of wimpy reporters. Punching a photographer, what's that? If you want to be bad, motherfucker, go to jail and try it. There are plenty of guys there who will kick your ass for a nickel and won't give a shit about it. It's all so fucking phony.'

I got onto the same subject with Rourke on a sunny afternoon in Toronto, 2002. 'Yeah, movie actors can be the least manly people in the fucking world when it comes right down to it,' he said. 'It can seem like a pretty silly profession for a man at times, wearing make-up and preening and posing. I never really confused that phony shit with acting. Acting can and should be about a lot more than that.'

I mentioned that he'd been one of the long list of next Brando/next Dean types. 'You know, I was a big fan of Brando,' said Rourke. 'But I never wanted to be the next Brando. I grew up digging Brando and Elvis and other guys like that, but the thing we see is the glory, we never see the shit, and there is always some shit behind the hype and the PR.'

The Nineties would see a rapid downward slide in the fortunes of Mickey Rourke. He was hang-

*Rourke as the intelligent hood formerly portrayed by Bogart, with Kelly Lynch as his compromised lawyer, in Michael Cimino's remake of* Desperate Hours *(1990).*

ing around with Hells Angels members, which alienated him from a lot of Hollywood people who, even by extension, didn't want any association whatsoever with biker gangs. He also had an entourage of flunkies surrounding him who did nothing but massage his ego and burn through his resources.

But, in the early Nineties, Rourke was still being offered studio projects, and, after the emotional experience of *Wild Orchid*, opted for the safe bet of working with one of his favourite directors, Michael Cimino. *Desperate Hours* would also reunite the Rourke-Cimino team with Dino De Laurentiis, as Rourke stepped into a role once played by no less than Humphrey Bogart. It's a remake of the 1955 film of the same name starring Bogart and Frederic March, itself based on a Broadway play by Joseph Hayes that won the playwright a Tony Award.

The story is one oft told in the pages of pulp crime novels, that of a criminal gang on the run who take refuge in a quiet neighbourhood, and terrorise the family whose home they have randomly selected. In the remake of *Desperate Hours*, the gang selects a family in a state of crisis that makes the volatility of their situation that much more pronounced.

Rourke plays a career criminal named Michael Bosworth, who charms his gorgeous blonde attorney (Kelly Lynch) with his suave demeanour and genius-level IQ into helping him escape from a court proceeding. He meets up with his brother (Elias Koteas) and another simpleminded criminal associate (David Morse), and they seek sanctuary in an affluent neighborhood. They select the home of a dysfunctional family headed by Anthony Hopkins and Mimi Rogers, the latter of whom is raising their two young children (Danny Gerrard and Shawnee Smith) on her own. (In the original film, the family unit is intact; in the remake, the father character has run off with a much younger woman, causing added friction.)

As with all his films, Cimino adds a special attention to detail that gives *Desperate Hours* a visual distinction. Shot in the wide open spaces and clean crispness of Utah, rather than looking like most other Hollywood movies (many of which are shot in Toronto), its unfamiliarity lends it a certain authenticity.

Rourke's performance is sharp and intense. His character is smart but cagey, seemingly suave, cool and calm, but he can erupt into instantaneous violence when provoked. Yet he projects an intelligence that gives his captives hope that he can be reasoned with. The scenes between Rourke, Rogers and Hopkins are a lot of fun, as all three actors approach their work so differently. I asked Sir Anthony Hopkins about his experience on *Desperate Hours* while interviewing him in New York City. 'I liked Mickey a lot, I like our interplay,' said Hopkins. 'What I liked about working with him is that he is very much in the moment as an actor, he reacts, he uses his gut to play each moment as real as he can. I would love to work with him again.'

The great Canadian actor Elias Koteas, who plays Rourke's brother Wally in the film, expressed similar sentiments. 'Mickey has a physical-ness, if that is a word, to his acting,' said Koteas. 'There were a few scenes that I remember doing that were rehearsed one way, but then he just exploded in a different direction, a very physical direction, and that then forced me to react to what was happening at that second rather than reacting the way that was rehearsed.'

Outside of his appearance in *Nine and a Half Weeks*, Mickey Rourke has rarely looked better than he did in *Desperate Hours*. He was trim and fit and his costumes were designer perfect. His performance was measured and layered, and he was totally convincing as a very smart guy who always chooses the criminal path, right to the end.

*Desperate Hours* was dumped into theatres on 2 October 1990, and disappeared quickly after grossing a few million dollars. The film itself has a blandness about it, as if the interesting components just never came together cohesively. Cimino is incapable of making a truly bad movie, but sometimes (as is the case with another Cimino film, *The Sicilian*) it feels like he's focusing on the minutiae and has lost sight of the big picture. With the exception of a strange film with Woody Harrelson called *Sunchasers*, Michael Cimino has not, to date, made any more films. He did write a novel that was published in France (*Big Jane*, Gallimard Books), but that has been his only visible creative output in recent years.

'I did one movie that made me feel like a complete fucking whore during that time,' said Mickey Rourke as we sat together on the balcony of his Toronto hotel suite. 'Can you guess which one that was?' I quickly ran through the Rourke canon in my head and arranged the titles according to their release date. '*Harley Davidson and the Marlboro Man*?' I offered. He smiled a painful smile and shook his head. 'You got it.' He took a long pull on a cigarette and gave another shake of the head. 'It wasn't just that I took the gig just for the money, it was the biggest payday I had ever had to that point, that made me feel like a total fucking whore, but the fact that the movie was such a complete piece of shit across the board made that even worse.'

*Harley Davidson and the Marlboro Man* first came to my attention well before the film was actually made. I was visiting a friend in Vancouver who was working on a cop series called *The Hat Squad*. During lunch breaks we would eat with the cast and crew, with the exception of the lead actor, who would eat in the corner by himself on the set while writing furiously on legal pads.

One day I asked this tall, friendly, blond actor, Don Michael Paul, what he was working on. 'I have a deal with MGM, I am working on a screenplay for them. Kind of a neo-Western road buddy heist movie set in the near future.'

Paul let me see a few of his completed pages, and it seemed to read like a *Butch Cassidy and the Sundance Kid* knockoff, but knocked way off. I asked Paul if he was writing this screenplay as an acting vehicle for himself. He replied that that would be a best case scenario, but he didn't have the pull to hold sway over a decision like that.

Eventually the film was packaged by the hapless MGM as a vehicle for a couple of cool bad boy actors – Mickey Rourke and the less reliable Don Johnson. That pairing in itself may not have been so bad at all, had it not been for an atrociously written script and a shaky director.

Simon Wincer is an Australian director who made a bit of a name for himself directing the epic TV mini-series *Lonesome Dove* (working with brilliant source material from Larry McMurtry). He also hired himself out to make such silly nonsense as *Crocodile Dundee in Los Angeles* and *The Phantom*. His complete and utter lack of style makes it look as if everyone involved in his films is just going through the motions.

As far as *Harley Davidson and the Marlboro Man* is concerned, 'going through the motions' may actually be a complimentary thing to say – after all, the alternative is to suggest that this piece of junk was the best that all involved could come up with.

The story is of two ageing drifters. All we know of them is that they have known each other a long time and one is called Harley (Davidson) because he rides a Harley Davidson motorcycle, and the other is called Marlboro (Man, one supposes) because he is a cowboy who smokes a lot. They meet up in a broken-down Burbank bar they both 'grew up' in, and find that the lease is about to expire and the bank is about to take it back. So Harley and Marlboro decide to commit a robbery to raise the outrageous amount of cash needed by their dear old friend, the bar owner. They rob an armoured car and find that the bags they ripped off were not filled with cash, but bricks of a new designer drug called Crystal Blue. Harley and Marlboro decide then to sell the drugs back to a corrupt banker. Once the switch is made, the banker (a svelte, suave looking Tom Sizemore) decides he doesn't like being played this way and sends his goons to retrieve his money. The beloved bar owner is killed in the shoot-out, causing Harley and Marlboro to seek out the banker and kill him in revenge.

In other words, there is a lot of mindless violence in this movie that serves no purpose at all. The cast, besides Rourke and Johnson, is on the weird side. A very young Daniel Baldwin plays the head of the goons (who wear ankle-length black leather dusters that make them utterly conspicuous). Tom Sizemore has a couple of nice moments, and Chelsea Field, a veteran TV actress who most recently starred in the series *Navy NCIS*, plays the female lead, doing the best she can with the limp material. Her character is called Virginia Slim (named after another American cigarette brand), and there is even a character called Jack Daniels (played by the late, hulking wrestling star Big John Studd).

When asked about Simon Wincer, Rourke turns vitriolic. 'He was a complete fucking bum. A real hack. Fuck man, this guy was letting Don Johnson tell him how to direct.' But the origins of this mess lie with the script, and whatever MGM studio executive thought it was worth several million dollars of production money. The film actually begins with a disclaimer, telling viewers that the title in no way indicates any form of endorsement of or by the products the characters are named after. What might in other circumstances have been a great promotional opportunity

*Poster for* Harley Davidson and the Marlboro Man *(1991), in which Rourke shared billing with Don Johnson. Both were on the way down; only one would re-emerge.*

had the named brands scrambling to disassociate themselves.

The writing is sophomoric and juvenile. Every line spoken by the two main characters has them calling each other Harley or Marlboro, as if there is something super cool about the names. The dialogue is even worse, cliché ridden, meaningless and misogynistic. (Women are referred to casually as 'bitches'.) Innocent people are constantly being indiscriminately shot, in displays of violence that have no real bearing on what might charitably be called 'the story'.

The bulk of the material is just so stupid, so ill thought-out, that it almost flies in the face of the old industry adage, 'No one sets out to make a bad movie.' The film went into production in 1991 and the story was set in 1996 – when, supposedly, the city of Burbank, California has gone through such a radical development that it is now a mega-metropolis with a major international airport, something that would take decades. And the robbery scene is a joke – an armoured car carrying a load of illegal drugs is diverted from its scheduled course four times, using nothing but plastic cones in the road – as is the ridiculously asinine catchphrase used throughout the film: 'It is better to be dead and cool than alive and uncool.'

Released on 23 August 1991, this film disappeared quickly from movie screens after a flurry of intensely negative reviews and almost total audience indifference. This indifference was right-eous, as this was probably the worst thing that Mickey Rourke has ever been a part of. There

*Rourke clutches his wound in generic thriller* White Sands *(1992). His small role is crucial to the plot, but the film almost became the swansong of his acting career.*

really is nothing redeemable about this film whatsoever.

From the way Rourke speaks about *Harley Davidson and the Marlboro Man*, it's often assumed that he walked out of the movie world and into the boxing ring directly after the experience. But, in fact, he had already signed up to play a small role in a crime thriller called *White Sands* before making the break. His role was small but significant, and his clout in Hollywood was still such that he was given the special credit 'and Mickey' in his own highlighted box.

In *White Sands* Rourke plays Gorman Lennox, who presents himself as an arms dealer but actually turns out to be a CIA operative. The film is on the routine side – a smalltime New Mexico lawman, Ray (the always reliable Willem Dafoe), has a murder on his hands, a man found dead beside an attache case filled with half a million dollars in cash. His investigation leads him to corrupt FBI agents and gunrunners, as Ray goes undercover as the dead man to see where the trail leads. The plot then gets very convoluted, when a rich young trust fund girl who arranged parties at her ranch to raise funds for rebellions and uprisings all over the world becomes inadvertently involved in the gunrunning deal. She brings the shadowy Gorman Lennox into it, as it seems the two have some kind of history together, which he will ultimately use against her as she falls for the married Ray under his assumed identity.

Rourke walks through the film. He does what he can to make his role interesting, but ultimately this is just another location shoot, another pay cheque, another job. He looks good and his lines are nowhere near as embarrassing as those he had to deliver in *Harley Davidson and the Marlboro Man*, but virtually any other actor on the scene at the time could have played this part just as well.

*White Sands* was directed by New Zealander Roger Donaldson, who has done better work in his day. He made an interesting thriller with Kevin Costner called *No Way Out*, and an underrated retelling of the Captain Bligh/Fletcher Christian story with *The Bounty*. His work on *White Sands* is interestingly visual, but it ends up feeling like just another Hollywood would-be-thriller to stick in the multiplexes and hope for the best. The storytelling has a journeyman-like blandness about it, although the supporting cast is interesting (Samuel L. Jackson and Mary Elizabeth Mastrantonio, of *Scarface*, as a corrupt FBI agent and the dilettante respectively).

I asked Roger Donaldson how Rourke became a part of the project, during a conversation in Los Angeles. 'I was always a big fan of Mickey Rourke's,' he said. 'I was delighted to have him in the film because he brought that rare combination of cool and dangerous intensity.' But, while everyone from Rourke on down did their jobs competently, there is nothing really memorable about the film. It was designed to be quickly disposed of in theatres, with the aim of recouping the money spent on it during its second life on home video.

By this time, Mickey Rourke had simply grown bored and disillusioned with Hollywood and moviemaking. He had a lot of passion for acting, and a lot of drive – but he was also saddled with a frustration by the filmmaking process that far outweighed it.

Did it make sense for him to simply walk away from acting? He has been asked this many times. 'You see, I didn't look at it as walking away from something,' he said. 'I looked at it as going back to something in my life that I had left unfinished and this just seemed like the perfect time to do it.'

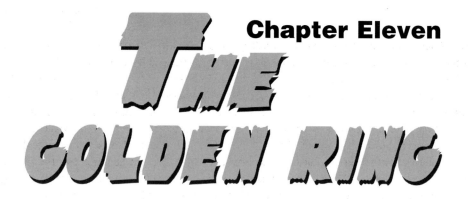

# Chapter Eleven

# THE GOLDEN RING

**'Go ahead, hit me again, see if I change.' –
Charlie Moran (Mickey Rourke),
The Pope of Greenwich Village**

Mickey Rourke has a small scar behind his ear. Not much of one really, but its origin is quite stark and telling. 'This is a little scar I got during one of my surgeries,' he said. 'They had to take a little piece of cartilage from behind my ear to use it to rebuild my nose.'

A lot has been written about Rourke's return to boxing as a professional fighter. Many refer to it as 'ill-fated', even though it was no worse than the experiences of the overwhelming majority of professional prize fighters. In the final retrospective analysis, there are, of course, a number of reasons why he probably shouldn't have made that decision at that time. But it was his way of fulfilling a dream, to do it because he felt that he *needed* to do it. And there is no one on the outside looking in who really has the right to challenge such a decision.

'I was a very athletic guy when I was a kid,' said Rourke. 'And while I was training and doing some boxing in Miami, long before being a professional actor hit me, it was my intention to turn pro as a boxer, to be a prize fighter. That was what I really wanted to do.' Rourke would elaborate on this in 1996, when he was shooting the lame sex thriller called *Exit in Red*. A Polish TV crew visited him on the set to make a documentary called *Mickey Rourke: Actor or Boxer?* He openly expressed how he knew his career switch might seem to be a folly to other people, but he really didn't care what they thought. 'I was looking for somewhere to run,' said Rourke. 'I wasn't going to get what I needed from a bottle or from drugs – boxing *was* my drug.' He would go on to clarify his mindset for the documentary makers. 'Boxing was something I did when I was young, I decided to do it again before I wasn't able to do it anymore. I did it and enjoyed it. The decision to do it professionally was based on a lot of things that were of the moment.'

The reasons why he probably should *not* have taken this path are twofold: the obvious one is the risk to his health during the bouts themselves, and the long-term neurological effects that repeated savage blows to the head inevitably have. The second reason is one of those quirks of Hollywood fate, how it can drop a stellar career into one person's lap after another has cast it aside.

In early 1993, when Quentin Tarantino was putting together what would become his magnum opus, *Pulp Fiction*, he had a fantasy of casting two actors who had slipped from their previous perches atop the Hollywood glory mountain: one was John Travolta, and the other Mickey Rourke.

Tarantino was a video-store clerk/geek/wannabe filmmaker who, with drive and talent, actually made his dreams of becoming a hip, successful filmmaker come true. One of his favourite films was the darkest of the earlier Travolta canon, Brian De Palma's *Blow Out*, and he was also a huge fan of Mickey Rourke – he mentioned once in an interview that, when he was a teenager, he wanted to *be* Mickey Rourke. Tarantino had the idea of casting Travolta in the role of Vincent Vega, the heroin-addicted hitman, and Rourke in the role of his nemesis, Butch Coolidge the boxer – a role that ultimately went to Bruce Willis, in one of the biggest strokes of casting luck in his life. It would gain Willis a credibility that he would cash in on but never match.

Tarantino's idea of casting Rourke in the film was well received by everyone who heard about it – all except Mickey Rourke, of course. Because Tarantino was such a huge fan, he knew of the passion for pugilism that made the role of a boxer on the wrong end of a fixed fight perfect, not only for Rourke's acting abilities but for his physicality as well.

But why did Rourke turn this role down? 'I don't know if I ever turned it down, not formally,' he said. 'I think I remember that I just never responded to the material at all after it was sent to me.' At the time the script was sent, he was in Kansas City preparing for a boxing match. Despite his cocksure attitude as a movie star, exuding cool and confidence, he was quite the opposite as a boxer. Before his professional fights, Rourke was filled with fear and anxiety. The movie role, any movie role, was the farthest thing from his mind. Now he looks back with a sardonic, hard-earned wisdom. 'Hey, I know, that was really stupid.'

When looked at now, it is hard to imagine anyone other than John Travolta in the Vincent Vega role. Conversely, it is easy to imagine any number of actors in the Butch Coolidge role. Bruce Willis is the personification of phony Hollywood tough-guy swagger, but Rourke could have brought dimensions to the character that Willis could not fathom even on his most inspired day.

A lot of observers portrayed Rourke's boxing career as some kind of early middle-aged folly, an attempt by a fading Hollywood tough guy to reassert his manhood. The facts of the matter reflect something quite different. Rourke was like the Leo Farnsworth character that Warren Beatty played in his delightful *Heaven Can Wait* – a guy giving the outward impression that he was a rich, eccentric fool, who bought the Los Angeles Rams so he could fulfil his fantasies of playing pro football as a quarterback. But all the while the heart and soul of an athlete lurked below the surface.

Those who actually mattered, the people in the fight game, took Mickey Rourke seriously as a boxer. It made no difference to them what Hollywood journalists and gossipmongers wrote. But his movie-star status just made things ten times more difficult for him. Opponents would naturally want to gain a little fame of their own, by putting the drop on a Hollywood tough guy.

But, once the decision was made, Rourke found that he actually had a couple of things working in his favour. He had been around fighters, trainers and boxing gyms for most of his youth, so he was familiar with the language of the fight game and knew what was expected of him. Nothing would blindside him. He had also amassed an impressive record as an amateur fighter, racking up 139 wins with just three losses. And his movie-star notoriety could be counted on to open a few doors that were inaccessible to other fighters early in their career, in terms of sponsorship and publicity.

It takes a lot of guts to step into a boxing ring in front of a large crowd, to face another professional boxer whose singular purpose in life is to beat the shit out of you. Most fighters train like demons because they have nothing else in their lives. But Rourke's idea of training differed from a lot of other fighters. As his friend, former boxing champion Ray 'Boom Boom' Mancini, said, 'I love Mickey, he is a great guy and a great friend, a real friend, but as a boxer, let's just say . . . he was a great actor.' Freddie Roach, Rourke's old trainer, described him as 'not a bad boxer, not great, there was nothing world class about him at all, but he could handle himself in the ring as he proved.'

And lest you think that Rourke's boxing career was a complete waste of time, consider this – it lasted just over three years and he fought in the super-middleweight class. In those three years he earned over $1.2 million in purse money. Not a bad haul in the real world.

Rourke's sparring partners included such dangerous fighters as James 'Lights Out' Toney, who once beat former heavyweight champion Evander Holyfield (after he'd lost the third of his world titles), and Carlos Monzon. Many of the injuries Rourke suffered during his boxing career happened in training, while sparring with these formerly top-ranked fighters.

Before he actually made his professional debut, he tuned up by fighting 24 amateur bouts. When Rourke had racked up an impressive twelve knockouts in a row he decided he was ready to turn pro.

Mickey Rourke made his professional boxing debut on 23 May 1991, in Fort Lauderdale, Florida. Rourke started the bout nervously and tentatively, found his stride in the third round, then had a great fourth that resulted in the decision going his way. His opponent was Steve Powell.

Watching his fights on tape, the Rourke you see in the ring is not the Rourke you are used to seeing in his movie roles. There is a nervousness and timidity to his movements, but, as in his acting, he had enough natural technique to overcome this. Part of what made Rourke's boxing career so tough on him physically was the fact that he had a hard time in training. Pro fighters train long and hard, with a determination to achieve a kind of personal perfection that is unwavering. When they have nothing left physically, they reach inside and find just a little bit more. Having just an ounce more stamina, and a physical toughness that slightly exceeds the other guy's, is what makes the difference in a professional fight.

As Freddie Roach said, 'Mickey is a tough guy, no doubt about that. But he had trouble getting into a training schedule that was steady. He hadn't lived that kind of life. Trying to get him up at 6:00 a.m. to do his road work [running] was impossible. We ended up having to go on midnight runs.' 'He should have made a kind of workout video for boxers,' chuckled 'Boom Boom' Mancini. 'He would do a bit of working out, then he would go have an espresso. Then some more working out for about fifteen minutes, then go have a cigarette. Then he would do a bit of heavy bag work, then he would go talk on the phone for a while.'

Rourke would take the nickname El Marielito, because it harked back to his days as a young boxer in Miami. Rourke had boxed in an area heavily populated by Cuban immigrants, who had mostly left Cuba from the Mariel Harbour – hence 'Marielitos'. He chose the moniker as a way of showing pride in his humble beginnings, associating himself with the community of Cubans he boxed with. He prepared himself for his pro boxing matches the same way that he prepared

*Mickey 'El Marielito' Rourke, complete with pencil moustache, prepares to square up to middleweight opponent Francisco Harris, in April 1992.*

himself for his films – on his own terms.

His boxing career spanned eleven fights contested all over the world, in places like the Bahamas, Argentina and Japan. While he was never defeated or knocked out, he did end up with a fractured and compressed cheekbone, broke bones in both hands, broke his nose a few times and suffered a few broken ribs. He also suffered a few concussions, one bad enough to jar his memory for over a week. It was this that would cause him to rethink his future as a prize fighter.

On 3 June 1992, Rourke knocked out Darrell Miller in the first round of their bout in Japan. On 20 November in Germany, he knocked out Thomas McCoy in three rounds. On 12 December 1993, in Spain, he knocked out Terry Jesmer in the fourth round. Mickey Rourke was no celebrity punch bag. He considers his best fight to be one he fought in Jamaica, a super-middleweight bout that was fought to a draw, but which he still considers the purest boxing of his brief career. Rourke officially retired from his career as a prize fighter in 1994. His last official bout was in Florida, against Steve Gibbons, ending in a split decision.

I asked Rourke about the day-to-day life of a boxer, what he thinks and feels as he heads into the ring. 'I'll tell you, man – in those moments right before the opening bell rung I was a bundle of nerves. Excited and adrenaline pumped for sure, but also very nervous, my mind racing all over the fucking place, trying to plan everything in my head I would do and what I would do if he did this or that . . . it was really a feeling of being electrically . . . alive,' he said.

Speaking to Rourke about his boxing career, there was a noticeable lack of flippancy, of tough guy talk. This is how he described his time leading up to a fight in 1994. 'It's a nightmare. I was scared shitless. It's frightening. Just pure fear. Total fucking fear. Once I get in the ring I am okay . . . it is just the four days leading up to a bout that I get the sweaty palms. When I was an amateur I had no fear. None at all. But as a pro . . . I think the fear came from the realisation that half the people there that came to see me fight came to see me lose.'

But, being Mickey Rourke, he still had to do things big. He once fought with bright, multicoloured trunks designed by Versace. 'Yeah, it was weird,' said Rourke. 'They announced Terry "the Hook" Jesmer in the red corner wearing the red trunks – then they announced Mickey "El Marielito" Rourke wearing the multicoloured Gianni Versace trunks . . . it made me feel a bit silly at the time. But after the tragedy [the murder of Versace in Miami] I was really glad that I hung onto them . . . they are an important keepsake now.'

And did his fear and anxiety play any part in his decision to stop boxing? 'Well it was more the fear of being permanently brain damaged than anything else. I had a lot of fights by this time, and I had won most of them. But it was the concussions . . . when a neurologist tells you that it might take a thousand more punches or it might take one more punch – but you are right on the edge of a major neurological event here, well let me tell you, brother, when I hear that, I fucking listen.'

Rourke credits Carre Otis with bringing his thinking around to his overall health and wellbeing. 'She was the first one to tell me that my speech was slurred,' he said. 'She was the first one to tell me that she had told me the same thing three times in a row.' Carre was also concerned about the number of sycophants who had latched on to him, and were making a good living off of him. These people included bikers and other fringe players, whom Rourke associated with because he thought them more authentic, more 'real' than Hollywood people – although, to his detriment, he would discover otherwise. He would often finance businesses for his 'friends' that ranged from hair salons and gyms to bars and cafés. Those who didn't have any business ambitions for Rourke to fund were employed by the production company he set up, Red Ruby Productions.

After his boxing career had ended, Rourke insisted, 'My doctor told me that I got knocked around so much that there is a gland in my head that isn't producing enough of whatever hormone that it produces which means that I can't have kids. Although they tell me that that will repair itself over time if I avoid head trauma.'

Rourke remained close to his boxing pals, even after his career as a professional fighter ended. 'These guys are my friends,' he said. 'I don't have a lot of actor friends, it's these guys that are my friends.' One such is three-time heavyweight champion of the world Evander Holyfield. Rourke accepted an invitation to visit Holyfield at his palatial Georgia estate just after his boxing career ended. The occasion was a special event organised by Holyfield in support of his children's charity, the Holyfield Foundation, attended by the cream of the boxing world past and present. Rourke was comfortable in their midst, joined at the event by his former boxing manager, Tony Holden. Asked to pay tribute to his pal Evander, he did so effusively and selflessly. Former middleweight champion of the world Sugar Ray Leonard was also in attendance, asserting, 'I've known Mickey Rourke for a long time and he is a great guy. He has always struck me more as a fighter, in terms of his inner self, than as an actor.'

One other boxer enthusiastically greeted Rourke because they had once fought on the same card together. Tommy Morrison is the grandson of the late Marion Morrison – also known as John Wayne – and starred alongside Sylvester Stallone in *Rocky V*. He and Rourke were like two old fraternity brothers of the ring.

Despite everything that has been said about Mickey Rourke's time as a professional boxer, he looks on it as a positive experience that ended up having some long-term negative effects. Rourke thought that he would end his boxing career and simply step back into acting, as if he'd been away on a long sabbatical. He would quickly and painfully discover that, once Hollywood shuts the door, you have to have a monumental amount of willpower, and more than a little luck, if you ever hope to push it back open again.

# Chapter Twelve

# WHERE DO YOU GO FROM HERE?

## The future isn't what it used to be, Mr. Angel.'
### – Louis Cyphre (Robert De Niro), Angel Heart

It wasn't as if Mickey Rourke had completely walked away from acting to pursue his boxing career. He would take small roles here and there, as long as the shooting schedules did not conflict with his training or his fight schedule. But it's true that, during this period, he no longer considered himself an actor – he was a prize fighter, and all his energies and concentration were devoted to that. And once he decided to go back to being an actor, he found that all that was left of his former career was a strangely negative reputation, and a deep-seated fear that most studios and filmmakers had of working with him.

There has been much speculation about the facial surgery that Rourke went through after his boxing career. It's certainly true that he'd suffered multiple facial fractures, with a number of them requiring reconstructive surgery. But that is not the entire story. When he was interviewed in 1996 for a travel show about New York City, Rourke looked trim and fit – most intriguingly though, his face looked like the Mickey Rourke of old. A few years older maybe, but nothing like the misshapen face he would present to the world shortly thereafter. He has repeatedly denied undergoing cosmetic surgery for reasons of vanity, and it has been confirmed that the operation on his compressed cheekbone and a reconstructive procedure on his nose took about seven hours apiece. But what happened to the rest of his face is probably only known by himself and his plastic surgeon, Dr. Robert Vitolo, MD.

But the altered state of his face was only one part of the larger problem. He could still get work, but the projects were less prestigious, and the money was a fraction of what he was getting a few years earlier. His lifestyle when things were riding high, and the leeches who surrounded him and lived off his salary, meant that Rourke actually needed to make those multimillion-dollar pay cheques just to keep the gears greased. He was living without the benefits of royalties on profitable films, endorsement deals, or other ancillary rights that pay some actors fat dividends long after they are considered has-beens.

None of this is to say that the work Rourke did during this low period was all bad, or that he had suddenly lost all his acting ability. The problem was that he had become saddled with a bad reputation since he was not around to defend himself, or counteract what was said about him.

One rumour was that he'd shown up to script meetings with some friends from the Hells Angels, flying full colours, whereas all that had happened was that some biker friends would visit him on set, in his trailer, now and again.

Rourke accepted a lot of roles in this period that he never would have touched during the high times. But in doing so, he forced himself to stretch as an actor. He would turn up in things like the video for Enrique Iglesias' song 'Hero', in which he played an intimidating tough guy opposite Iglesias' sensitive hero. (The standard response to the video was, 'Oh yeah, Mickey Rourke, whatever happened to him?')

He would also accept a role in a weird little film alternatively known as *F.T.W. (Fuck the World)* or *The Last Ride*, which also bears his name in the writing credits (or at least his assumed name of Sir Eddie Cook). Rourke stars in the film as Frank Wells, a guy just getting out of prison after a long stretch for manslaughter. He tries to return to his old life as a talented rodeo rider, but he meets a young woman and falls hard for her. The fact that she happens to be an armed bank robber on the run causes Frank's life to go into another unexpected tailspin.

Rourke was surrounded by a truly talented and eclectic group of actors who make the film fun to watch, even though it is decidedly uneven, including Aaron Neville, the burly African-American singer with the voice of an angel, Lori Singer, Peter Berg and Native American actor Rodney *(Dances with Wolves)* Grant. The director, Michael Karbelnickoff, was a veteran of Zalman King's *Red Shoe Diaries* series, and the film was co-written by Mari Kornhauser, who wrote the erotic *Zandalee*. Rourke once again plays an unapologetic outsider on the fringes of society, and the film is uneven as a lot of its twists and turns seem a bit improbable. But the acting is uniformly interesting, the photography is always engaging, as the film was shot in the picturesque Western state of Montana, and there is a decent music score. The film got a theatrical release in Germany on 6 April 1995, and was released in Argentina for a week or so, but was dumped onto VHS and DVD for the rest of the world. Even though not a lot was expected of this film, Rourke took his work seriously and it shows.

Rourke then accepted a starring role in a film for HBO called *The Last Outlaw*. It was the first Western he had appeared in since *Heaven's Gate* and, like that film, was decidedly hampered by its slow pacing. It was another case of Rourke in an interesting movie, with a terrific cast and a lot of talent behind the camera, that just never seemed to come together and never found an audience. He stars in the film as a Civil War colonel named Graff, who leads some of his ragtag cohorts on a violent robbery spree. When his gang betray him, Graff surrenders to the authorities and offers to help track them down. He is of course planning to exact revenge while under the protection of the law, and then to escape custody once he has completed his task.

Shot in rugged New Mexico, this film has that dusty, gritty look that brings to mind the Westerns of Sam Peckinpah. It was directed by New Zealander Geoff Murphy, who was known for his early films *Goodbye Pork Pie* and *The Quiet Earth*, before hitting the Hollywood gravy train and churning out stuff like *Young Guns 2, Under Siege 2* and *Fortress 2*. The screenplay is pretty good, courtesy of Eric Red who has written such horror genre favourites as *The Hitcher, Near Dark* and (an underrated guilty pleasure) *Body Parts.*

*The Last Outlaw* is not a great film, but it is solid. It co-stars Dermott Mulroney, Steve Buscemi (who would later cast Rourke in a film he was directing) and Keith David, and is worth checking out on DVD. Contemporary American Westerns tend to be revisionist in nature, but this film unfolds with the simplicity of the old-time Hollywood Westerns. There are bad guys and good guys, sometimes the good guys turn bad and the bad guys turn good, everyone and everything in the film is dusty, there are lots of gunfights, and the morality is only a few shades darker than the morality of the traditional Western. There are a few moments that feel like direct homages to classic Westerns, with an opening bank robbery sequence that might have been devised by Peckinpah himself. But because the film unfolds at a very laconic pace, it probably seems quite gruelling for a modern audience raised on video games.

During the next two years, 1995-97, Rourke would work on whatever he could. His personal life was a shambles; he was barely hanging onto his troubled relationship with Carre Otis, who was having serious drug problems at the time. Rourke's money problems were mounting monthly. No matter how much work he was getting, it simply wasn't paying him enough. Rourke found himself back where most actors are at the beginning of their careers: struggling to make the rent, and taking any acting role that comes along.

Next up was a co-starring role in an independent film called *Fall Time*. It was the start of a pattern that would repeat itself often throughout the low years. Young filmmakers putting together a small feature were looking to cool up their cast, and contacted Mickey Rourke about being in their film. He was in no position to turn any work down at this time, and was happy for their attention.

In this case the filmmakers were Steve Alden and Paul Skemp, who wrote the script, and Paul Warner, who directed the film. It's about a trio of young men (Jason London, David Arquette and Jonah Blechman) who plan a mock kidnapping of another young man, played by Stephen Baldwin. But their mock crime coincidentally crosses paths with a real bank robbery planned by a couple of ex-cons, led by a softly spoken malevolent force by the name of Florence (Rourke). German-born actress Sheryl Lee – who gained some notoriety from her work for David Lynch on *Wild at Heart* and the TV show *Twin Peaks* – plays the female lead but isn't given a lot to do. This dark comedy seems to be more about the homosexual undertones between the young men and the ex-cons and their victim.

Rourke wasn't required to stretch himself much for this film – he is likeable and watchable as always, but his role is nothing but tough guy lines whispered in a threatening manner. Baldwin, on the other hand, displays a humanity and fearful sensitivity unlike anything he's played before.

The film got a very limited theatrical release in July 1995, and then another very brief theatrical opening in Hungary the following April. Once again, Mickey Rourke's efforts were on display in North America only if you sought them out at your local video store.

This would also be the case with his next film, a starring role in a lurid sex thriller called *Exit in Red*. Rourke stars as a psychiatrist who moves out west to escape some sexual misconduct charges that his gorgeous female attorney gets him off of. The sexual intrigue from hereon in gets so convoluted that it is actually hard to follow. Rourke's attorney has a big thing for him but it is unrequited. He then falls for a woman who is a little disturbed herself, and their affair turns weird when her husband finds out. She calls Dr. Rourke one night to tell him her husband has gone crazy and beaten her. He rushes to her side, only to find that she has killed her husband in self defence – except this wasn't the real husband, but a lover pretending to be him, before both lovers run off and leave Rourke to take the fall for the real husband's genuine death. Because of his chequered past, Dr. Rourke cannot convince the authorities that he really had nothing to do with the crime. So he must settle the matter quickly on his own, using any means available to him.

If this film is notable at all, it's because it saw the re-pairing of Rourke and his wife, Carre Otis, but there is nothing like the sparks of eroticism the pair captured in *Wild Orchid*. Rourke looks interesting, his face having obviously undergone some alteration since his last appearance on film, sporting long blond hair and dressed like a pimp who dabbles in psychiatry on the side. He has a few interesting lines, and his confrontation scenes with the jealous lover (played with manic, spitting intensity by Anthony Michael Hall) are very interesting, as are his interrogation scenes. But the erotic scenes in the film are quite limp.

The film was directed by Polish-born filmmaker Yurek Bogyayevicz and written by David Womark, a first assistant director turned screenwriter who also made a couple of *Red Shoe Diaries* episodes, with assistance by J. S. Cardone. It was obviously their attempt to construct a dangerous, sexually charged thriller, but it just ends up being tedious and confusing.

From here, Rourke went straight into a film that connected him with a co-star who quickly became a close friend, although their friendship would end in tragedy. The film was called *Bullet*, and his co-star was Tupac Shakur.

Of all the films Rourke made at his low point, this one deserves some attention. While it does tend towards predictability at times, it is a grittily harsh, uncompromising look at life on the streets, made by a director actually in possession of a certain artistry.

Rourke stars as Butch 'Bullet' Stein, a Jewish heroin addict just released from prison after an eight-year stretch. The film follows his day-to-day life, as he heads back to the streets and reunites with his old pals and his brothers, and gets right back into the life that dropped him in prison all those years before. One of his first actions is to rip off a courier for a local drug lord named Tank (Shakur), who vows swift and violent revenge both for this act of disrespect and for those still pending from the past. Rourke finds himself adrift, with only a few people willing to stand by his side: his best friend, Lester (John Enos III), and his brothers, Louis (Ted Levine), a Vietnam veteran with a fractured psyche, and Ruby (future Academy Award winner Adrien Brody), a young man with dreams of becoming an artist.

*Bullet* was shot in some tough locations in and around New York City, including Sing Sing Prison in Ossining, Cypress Hills Cemetery in Brooklyn, and Coney Island. The director was the enormously talented and innovative British filmmaker Julien Temple, who first came to prominence in 1980 with the resonant punk-era film *The Great Rock 'n' Roll Swindle*. He went on to work with some of the great names in popular music on their trendsetting videos (Van Halen's 'Jump', David Bowie's 'Jazzin' for Blue Jean' and Whitney Houston's 'I'm Your Baby Tonight' among them), and has made some musical feature films (*Earth Girls Are Easy*, *Absolute Beginners*). But there was something raw and interesting about the screenplay for *Bullet* that gave Temple the chance to tell a story from the underbelly of America, the America that no one gets to see unless you are one of the unfortunate dwellers of that netherworld. Temple's work in *Bullet* is hard to fault in any area. He gets solid performances from his actors and uses his camera like a kind of dark mirror. This is a dark and depressing film, but at the same time so penetrat-

**103**

ing and well made that it's surprising it didn't gain a lot more attention.

Rourke is very good in the film, for which he also helped write the script and served as music supervisor. His performance is not just the standard tough guy/ex-con/loser, as he manages to carve some additional dimensions into his characterisation. He co-wrote the film with Bruce Rubenstein (who wrote a TV biopic of Jimi Hendrix), once again under the pseudonym Sir Eddie Cook. When asked about the origin of the moniker, Rourke tells the story of how he was on the run from the cops when he was a kid. He and a friend had just boosted some candy from a local theatre. The other kid was caught and very quickly ratted Mickey out. 'When they grabbed me and asked me my name I just blurted out that my name was Eddie Cook because I remembered it from a rhyme.'

This film also marked the last screen performance of rapper Tupac Shakur, who would be fatally shot in Las Vegas in September 1996, allegedly as a result of a turf war between the East and West Coast hip-hop scenes. Rourke and Shakur would form an instant bond. Rourke believed that Shakur was a lot like himself, pegged as this terrible guy with a horrific reputation, even though he only thought of himself as a poet, writer and musician. Shakur's death would rattle him to the core. To this day, Rourke still keeps a picture of the rapper displayed prominently in his home.

*Bullet* actually did make it into theatres in North America for a very limited run in October 1996, and was released on home video the following June. The version currently available on DVD is unrated, delving deeper and more darkly into the story than the initial R-rated version.

Just after filming was completed, gossip columnist A. J. Benza (*New York Daily News*) had a late night experience with Rourke. Another New York City columnist named Richard Johnson was making a side career out of slamming Rourke – everything from frequent and pointless remarks about his grooming and dress sense to dubious reports of Rourke being spotted in a gay bar, trying to pick up young men. One night Rourke decided he had had enough.

'I get this call from Mickey Rourke at about 3:30 in the morning,' said Benza. 'And he is mad as hell, he wants me to tell him where Richard Johnson lives so he can go have a talk with him. He told me that he was down at a bar called Frederick's with Tupac. I told him I would be right down. When I get there Tupac is at the bar and Mickey is in the restroom with a copy of the newspaper with Johnson's column in it that he found so offensive and he was in a bad mood, a bad, bad mood. He was literally beating the shit out of the bathroom. He was fuming that Johnson had been making fun of his relationship troubles with Carre Otis in the column. I had to talk him out of tearing Johnson apart.'

Rourke got caught up in another little public spat, this time with Mel Gibson, after he made a comment about acting not being a particularly manly occupation (something that Brando, Jimmy Dean, Paul Newman and Steve McQueen had all said before him). Gibson decided to take Rourke to task, saying, 'That's just Mickey talking – he likes to think that he is a tough guy in a black t-shirt.' When Rourke heard Gibson's comment, he shot back, 'Well Mel, I am.'

Rourke once again wound up on the bad end of some newsprint when he showed up at the trial of Mob boss John Gotti, who was being tried for racketeering and murder in New York City. There was speculation that Rourke was researching a role, but that was not the case. (Armand Assante ended up playing Gotti in a made for TV movie.) 'I'm just here supporting a friend,' was

*Rourke with his friend and co-star from* Bullet *(1996), Tupac Shakur. The actor empathised with the gangsta rapper and was saddened by his murder.*

all he would say when a reporter shoved a microphone in his face.

To describe Rourke and Gotti as 'friends' is a little on the grandiose side – though they had met a number of times in New York hotels, and often had dinner in the same places. But there was clearly an element of Mickey Rourke that wasn't averse to grabbing some street credibility at such a notorious event.

During this period, Rourke was dividing his time between New York City, which he described as 'the place I feel most alive in,' and a small bungalow in the Hollywood Hills, which he referred to as 'that other place'. In New York he lived in a series of hotels, and later an apartment that was decorated to look and feel like a hotel. 'When people come here I don't want there to be anything here that says, "Mickey Rourke lives here,"' he explained.

One of the more ridiculous choices Rourke made during this period was agreeing to co-star in a noisy, gimmicky martial arts film called *Double Team*. His co-stars were Jean Claude Van Damme and basketball star/media freak Dennis Rodman, in this story of futuristic counter-terrorism in which Rourke played a heavy named Stavros.

*Double Team* producer Moshe Diamant said they were looking for someone who was not typically cast as a bad guy or a terrorist. 'Mickey Rourke's name came up and I thought the choice was interesting,' said Diamant. 'So we set up a meeting and within minutes I was thinking to myself that this was our Stavros. You see a different side to Mickey Rourke in this movie. He has a lot of energy and power, and a lot of charisma too.' The film was written by Dan Jakoby, who contributed to the story of the 1986 sci-fi sequel *Aliens*, and directed by Hong Kong action producer/director Tsui Hark, who made his name in the Eighties producing some of the original ultraviolent gangster films directed by John Woo, such as *A Better Tomorrow*.

The film was backed by Columbia Pictures and designed as simple action fodder for audiences in North America, but also to make a killing overseas where Van Damme was still a draw. Since Rourke would be called on to engage in a climactic battle scene with Van Damme at the end of the film, he went into serious physical training with martial arts instructors so that it would have a look of authenticity about it (though the rest of the film is patently unrealistic). Because of this, Mickey Rourke looked physically better than he had in any film since *Nine and a Half Weeks*.

In fact, all involved seemed to take it deadly seriously. After going through all the rigorous training, Rourke would say bemusedly, 'I used to look down on this kind of film but you have to have a tremendous amount of concentration to do this work – the same as if you were doing Shakespeare. A moment of lost concentration can really cause you to hurt someone – it's very physically demanding. But I enjoyed that aspect of it because it kept me focused. I haven't had a chance to be bored on this film because they have kept me so fucking busy.'

*Double Team* was shot in France and Rome, which is another reason why Rourke agreed to do the film. But beyond that, the movie has freak show written all over it. Dennis Rodman was a pretty good basketball player, during his career with the Chicago Bulls and the Los Angeles Lakers, but his presence in the film – with the garish tattoos that cover his body and his rainbow-dyed hair – reduces it to a pop-culture joke. Tsui Hark made such a silly film that it even looked beneath the talents of Jean Claude Van Damme.

The story is preposterous. Van Damme plays Jack Quinn, a government-sponsored assassin charged with killing the evil Stavros. This is to be Quinn's final mission, but Stavros outwits him and Quinn is sent to the high-tech Colony – a secret hiding place for agents to have their identities erased, get retrained and be sent back out into the field under fresh new identities. But Quinn has a score to settle, he wants Stavros now, and devises a way to break out of the Colony with the help of a guy named Yaz (Rodman), as physically conspicuous an arms dealer as can be imagined. But Stavros, who seems to be omniscient, knows what is to come and targets Quinn's pregnant wife, Katherine, as a hostage to keep him at a safe distance. It all leads to a final battle in Rome with lots of martial arts fighting, many explosions and a tiger all figuring in the action.

The budget for *Double Team* was considerable for an action movie, about $30 million. Columbia Pictures assured a major release (over 2,000 theatres on the weekend of 6 April 1997), but the film failed to grab that all-important action audience and only pulled in a sparse $5 million during its opening weekend. It made just over $11 million during its domestic theatrical run, but pulled in another $40 million in theatres around the world, making a profit in the long run.

In 1997 a sequel to *Nine and a Half Weeks* would be made, quickly and with very little artistic justification. Just about everyone involved in the original film had stated that they thought studio pressures had caused it to be less than it was intended to be. For a while, it was assumed that by making a sequel they could correct the missteps made during the original, and finally make the film they wanted.

For a short while, about ten years prior to the actual making of the sequel, Roman Polanski was very keen on making the film. Some preliminary writing and development commenced for a film to be called *Two Weeks in Paris*. It stalled when it appeared that the same creative problems that caused the first film to get lost in a fog were manifesting for the second time around.

Years would go by as the fortunes of those involved with the original film ebbed and flowed. By 1996, Kim Basinger was an Oscar winner (for *LA Confidential*) and had made a fortune, for some reason spending most of it on buying a small town in Minnesota, which sent her bankrupt. Mickey Rourke was flat on his ass by this time, and willing to talk to anyone about any project at all. The idea of doing a sequel to the most popular film he had ever made seemed like just the ticket.

The intentions going into this sequel were solid, not as exploitative as some might think – downright ambitious, in fact. The director was one of the best editors in film, Ann Goursaud. Her list of credits as an editor was impressive – *Ironweed*, *The Two Jakes*, *Bram Stoker's Dracula*, *The Outsiders*, amongst many others – but her work as director was limited to dabbling in the soft-core erotic series *Red Shoes Diaries*. Still, she knew her way around the filmmaking process and was comfortable in directing erotica – so she seemed to be a perfect choice to direct *Another Nine and a Half Weeks* (aka *Love in Paris*).

Irish writer Mick Davis came up with a story set in Paris. John Gray (Rourke – who now has a last name for his character) goes to Paris to track down Elizabeth, who fled there after their break-up in New York. He connects with a darkly mysterious fashion designer named Lea and her assistant Claire, who, it turns out, was a friend of Elizabeth's while she was in Paris.

John is told that Elizabeth married a man she met in Paris, and has since left. Then things begin to develop between him and the sultry Lea, until he becomes suspicious upon hearing about the real circumstances of Elizabeth's leaving from Lea's business partner, Vittorio.

There are a couple of things that drag this movie down like a lead weight. One is the fact that Rourke looks rougher than hell – several hundred miles of rough road from the elegant, suave John of the original film. At that time he had gone through a certain amount of facial surgery, initially attributed to repair work on injuries sustained during his boxing career. But Rourke had done television interviews just after giving up boxing, and his face looked fine at that time. The face in the film displays the telltale signs of cosmetic surgery, which may have been performed over the long term – or may have gone rather horribly wrong.

The second big drawback is the exceedingly wooden acting of former model Angie Everhardt. She is fantastic to look at, but this is a story about love lost, longing, regret and dread. To pull that off, you need actors who are comfortable exposing their emotions as well as their bodies.

I asked screenwriter Mick Davis for his thoughts on the casting when he was at the 2004 Toronto International Film Festival, promoting his film *Modigliani*: 'I think you are right in saying that the casting was a major . . . problem,' hesitated Davis. 'Indeed, Mickey Rourke was not the Mickey Rourke of old – and I am not just referring to his physical appearance either. When he played this guy ten years previous he was full of confidence and attitude and he knew he looked great. By this time around he had been through some shit, he wasn't quite so confident, and he knew he didn't look so hot. And the casting of the female lead was strange too, I am sure they could have found someone who could have pulled the role off quite easily, a French actress was my idea, they are willing to try anything in a role. But going the model route weakened the overall film considerably.'

But even at this low point, virtually everyone that Rourke worked with had nothing but positive things to say about him.

French co-star Agatha De La Fontaine said, 'I never met such a charming man. He has a wonderful aura about him and he has the most cheeky smile.' Angie Everhardt described her working experience on the film: 'It was the second day on the set. And I've been friends with Mickey for nine years. He is such a method actor – he looks right into your eyes and his stare is very intense. All of a sudden I got so nervous that I couldn't remember my lines, my address, my phone number. I almost fainted I was so intimidated. Mickey Rourke is a great fucking actor. All of a sudden it wasn't Mickey Rourke my friend, but *Mickey Rourke!* I was terrified.'

Everhardt went on to offer up her general opinion of her friend: 'I think the spotlight can be a very lonely place to be. Everyone always seems to want something from you, pulling at you. I think he's a bit lonely. I think Mickey has had some ups and downs that have hit him pretty hard.'

There is nothing really positive to say about *Another Nine and a Half Weeks/Love in Paris* – except that the idea of making a sequel to the original film was not a bad one, and had Polanski followed through on his plans it could have been very interesting indeed.

But what we have is a mess of the highest order. Mickey Rourke has never looked worse in a film before or since. He may even have looked better on the surgeon's table, with his face laid open during the corrective surgery on his compressed and fractured cheekbone. Add to that the banal but overreaching script, which was trying to say some things that really belonged in another film, and the total lack of chemistry with his co-star. But it could have been worse – as illustrated by the ingenious idea of mounting a 'prequel' to *Nine and a Half Weeks* and calling it *The First Nine and a Half Weeks*, which showed John as a young guy (Australian actor Paul Mercurio), identifying within himself the impulses to exert control over personal and sexual encounters.

During this time, Rourke received some much needed moral support and mentoring from Irish actor Richard Harris. Rourke and Harris had never actually worked together, but had met a while before when they were staying in the same Irish hotel. Harris liked Rourke a lot, and had been to a lot of the same dark places. I asked Harris about this shortly before his death, in an interview in Toronto. 'Mickey is a good guy, deep down he is a good person, a man's man,' said Harris. 'And because of that, because of his innate sensitivity he was taken advantage of by all those whom had sucked good livings out of his efforts only to desert him when things turned bad. I had been down that road myself and I know how painful that realisation is and how difficult that position is to be in. I could help him. I wanted to help him.'

Harris would arrange for a house for Rourke to live in once his marriage to Carre Otis finally went up in smoke – when he lost his home, and most of his possessions. Because of this support, Rourke was in a positive enough state of mind to appreciate the ray of sunshine that would finally burn through the clouds.

# Chapter Thirteen
# BRUISER

## 'A wise man can see more from the bottom of a well than a fool can see from a mountaintop.' – *Julius Caesar*

'Francis called me up and asked me if my hair was still dyed blonde, like it was in the movie,' said Mickey Rourke. 'I told him that it was and asked him why he was asking me that – he said that after the test screenings for the film the audiences all said they wanted to see more of my character. So Francis wrote some extra stuff and we shot it. I really appreciated that Francis was giving me this kind of a shot, more than I can even put into words.'

The movie was *The Rainmaker*, based on the bestselling John Grisham book. And the director was Francis Ford Coppola.

In May 2001, I had the chance to speak to Coppola about the casting of Rourke in *The Rainmaker*. We were seated under a tent on a warm afternoon at the Cannes International Film Festival in France. Coppola was there to unveil his recut *Apocalypse Now Redux*. He was wearing khaki pants and a loose fitting, flowered shirt, and was relaxed and talkative. 'On *Rumble Fish* I needed a guy like Mickey,' said Coppola. 'I needed a really intense actor, not just that kind of *actor* intensity, but a guy with a kind of crazy fire in his eyes, a guy that you could never second guess. And that was what Mickey brought to the movie. But with *Rainmaker* I needed a kind of gruff guy, a weathered, been-around-the-block guy who also had a kind of earned wisdom that also meant you underestimated him at your own peril. And at that time in his life and career, that was also Mickey.'

The character of Bruiser Stone in Coppola's big budgeted film for a big studio (Paramount) with a hot young leading actor (Matt Damon) was precisely what Rourke needed at that point in his life and career. It wasn't that he had lost his abilities, but he felt he needed just one prestigious filmmaker to take a chance on him without fear of the baggage he carried.

'Francis went out on a limb for me with *Rainmaker*,' said Rourke with a knowing smile and a shake of the head. 'And I knew it too, so I gave the role every fucking ounce of effort that I had in me. And it turned out well, better than I think we all expected. I owe Francis and will always feel a special kind of gratitude towards him.'

Rourke embraced the opportunity, opening himself up to the experience. 'I really enjoyed making this film,' he said. 'The last time I had this much fun making a film was when I did *The Pope of Greenwich Village*. Francis is in complete control of his sets and everyone around him knows it. That lends a lot of confidence and comfort to a set.'

When I asked Coppola about the mechanics of getting Rourke involved in the film, he said with a chuckle, 'It was actually quite funny because when I was doing the prep for the film I kept hearing from the studio guys that I should be on the lookout for a "Mickey Rourke type" of a guy for the Bruiser Stone role. I kept telling them that *the actual* Mickey Rourke was still around and he was still acting and he would be perfect for the Bruiser role, so even though I was agreeing with what they were demanding, they still fought me on him.'

Thanks to a clever piece of narration written by Michael Herr, we are introduced to the Bruiser Stone character slightly ahead of seeing him. Then we see him dressed in a dapper gameshow host suit, with white-ish hair and a salt and pepper goatee, looking smooth and cool but rough and weatherbeaten at the same time. Rourke made an instant impression on the audience.

The story concerns a young law student named Rudy Baylor (Damon) who has just been evicted from his apartment before he has to take his bar exams. Rudy finds a job with an ambulance-chasing law firm run by the gravel-voiced Bruiser Stone, and begins gathering cases. One involves a young woman (nicely played by Clare Danes) being horribly abused by her bullying husband. And the second involves a young man dying of cancer, who is being denied benefits by the greedy insurance company with whom his mother had arranged a policy. With Bruiser on the run from racketeering charges, Rudy is left to fight this case along with a junior partner named Deck Shiffler (Danny DeVito), who is not technically a lawyer. They are up against a multi-partnered, big-money law firm, headed by a slickly condescending lawyer (a good performance by Jon Voight). But in this case, idealism wins out over avarice – not actually something that happens often in the real world, but it makes for a powerfully uplifting ending to a movie. John Grisham has described it as his favourite of all the screen adaptations of his work thus far.

'The funny thing was that after I fought like hell to get Mickey onboard and after he did so well in the first few scenes, then all those same people who were trying to dissuade me from casting him were all telling me to expand and deepen his role so he would be onscreen more often,' said Coppola.

While a little on the long side, *The Rainmaker* is a thoroughly enjoyably courtroom drama that Rourke steals outright with his performance as the shrewd lawyer with the lounge-lizard ways. His office is filled with assistants and secretaries who all look like they just stepped out of the latest VividVideo XXX release. Rourke's costumes, and his malevolent delivery of even the most inconsequential lines, make for a memorable performance that provides a kind of unintended (but perfectly valid) comic relief.

The film was well received by critics. From a budget of $40 million, it would earn well over $50 million during its domestic theatrical release, with another $46 million coming from foreign territories and another $20 million in video sales.

But even though Rourke was frequently highlighted in those postive notices, and the film was a popular hit with audiences, he still found that he was on the outs with most studios and A-list filmmakers. So he went right back to accepting roles in little films, working with filmmakers who cast him pretty much so that they could meet Mickey Rourke. There was the odd exception, but the next couple of years would once more be a time of struggle, self-doubt, and even despair.

After the rush of *The Rainmaker*, Rourke appeared as a fourth billed player (his character was called the Bookie) in a pretentious piece of indie bullshit called *Buffalo 66*, from writer/director/'star' Vincent Gallo. Gallo tends to attach himself to artists a hundred times more accomplished than he is, like Johnny Depp and Mickey Rourke (or, further back, troubled, mercurial visual artist Jean Michel Basquiat), as part of his strutting, posing self-aggrandisement. He would later prove himself to be the one of the masters of self-absorbed cinematic onanism, with his ridiculously boring *The Brown Bunny* (which, to be fair, makes *Buffalo 66* look like *Citizen Kane*).

*As Bruiser Stone, with Matt Damon in* The Rainmaker *(1997). Rourke was cast as the shifty attorney by Francis Ford Coppola, one of the directors who rescued his career.*

In *Buffalo 66*, Gallo cast himself as a guy who has just been released after a five-year prison term, only to realise that life on the outside is not something he can cope with anymore. He kept the fact he was in prison from everyone, including his parents, who thought he was living a successful life somewhere with his new wife. While on the road in Buffalo, and in need of a restroom, he ducks into a dance studio and then decides to kidnap one of the students to force her to pretend she is his wife.

Besides Rourke, Gallo did manage to cast some great actors for the film. Christina Ricci plays his pretend wife, and Anjelica Huston and Ben Gazzara play his parents. But even they can't save the film from that look-how-cool-I-am school of American independent self-indulgence. It's Gallo's M.O. to attach himself like a barnacle to really talented people and fill his films with arty pretence. He cast Rourke in this mess because he wanted to rub elbows with him (and Gazzara, for that matter), claiming, 'when Mickey Rourke appeared on the set of my little $1.5 million movie everyone looked toward him and there was a kind of respectful hush that settled over the set.' Rourke did one day's work on the film and took the cash that Gallo allotted him. He only appears briefly in his role as a dark and mysterious bookie, and is not very memorable.

One of the more interesting projects that Rourke attached himself to during this low time was a made-for-cable film called *Thicker than Blood*, in which he played a Catholic priest in New York City trying to save the souls – in fact, the very lives – of some street kids in his parish. Virtually every review of this film mentioned how odd it was to see Mickey Rourke playing a priest. The fact that Rourke was raised a Catholic, and remains surprisingly devout to this day, seems to have escaped these writers. His performance as Father Frank Larkin is disciplined and precise, a nice piece of understated acting from a guy who usually uses his intense emotions to explode outward, rather than releasing them in tightly controlled bursts. (Co-starring in *Thicker than Blood* was a young actor named Dan Futterman, who would earn an Academy Award nomination for his first ever produced screenplay, *Capote*.)

While this was pretty much a standard TV movie, it proved that Rourke still possessed the spark that allowed him to delve deep into a character, to connect with the material on a passionate level. He had never walked away from Hollywood *per se*, although he was sick of the Hollywood system. But he was still an actor at heart. He would tell an interviewer at the time, 'You know, some of these Hollywood producers, they want to own you, own your soul. And there are plenty of guys out there who are more than willing to sell it to them. But if you choose not to then you find yourself on the wrong end of a bad reputation.'

Rourke would follow this up with another quickie appearance, in a low-budget indie film with Tarantino-esque aspirations called *Thursday*. He does not show up until almost the end, but what comes before that is an earnest little attempt at a neo-*noir* crime thriller. Once again Rourke is cast as a meanie, this time named Khasarov, and surrounded by a uniformly good cast: Thomas Jane, Aaron Eckhardt, Paulina Porizkova and future *CSI* star Gary Dourdain.

This film was obviously influenced by Quentin Tarantino, but the writer-director, Skip Woods, would go on to write the big-budget John Travolta vehicle *Swordfish* and write and direct the Vin Diesel film *Hitman*. Someone obviously saw *Thursday* and figured this was a guy on the rise, and it succeeds on a lot more levels than it fails.

I asked Rourke about this time in his life, and he said immediately that he was done with that kind of thing. But what kind of thing, exactly? 'You know, that stuff where I do some meetings with directors just because they want to meet me,' said Rourke. 'Now, if you want to meet with me you better have something in the way of work that you want to offer me or don't waste my fucking time. I'm trying to get seriously connected to the work again so I am not interested in film geeks who just want to meet Mickey Rourke. I used to do that because I had nothing else to do, but things are different now.'

Rourke's next role was in another ultraviolent action film, *Point Blank*, which is certainly not to be confused with the classic thriller of the same title from 1967 starring Lee Marvin. It's a quickly dashed-off affair about a group of very dangerous criminals in Texas, who are released back onto the street just as violent and psychotic as when they went inside. They arm themselves and terrorise an entire shopping mall, and, since they are all bent on destruction and mayhem anyway, there is no way to reason with them. This is where the ever-reliable rogue cop character arrives to do battle with the bad guys. Rourke growls, shoots and hits people as he walks through

*As the bad guy in* Thursday *(1998), an indie thriller with Tarantino-esque aspirations. Rourke was later cast in films by Tarantino himself, and collaborator Robert Rodriguez.*

the film with no real effort or distinction. He did get his name above the title, but that was an obvious ruse to sell the overseas rights. There are some interesting talents involved in the movie, but director Matt Earl Beesley isn't one of them. Danny Trejo, an ex-con himself in real life, is the most effective of the bad guys, but, all in all, this movie belongs in the sale bins of video stores.

By this time in 1998, Rourke's marriage to Carre Otis was all but done for. They would divorce that December. In 1999, it would be reported that Carre had a seizure while working, and a subsequent operation discovered three small holes in her heart. Her heart was reportedly 'partially collapsed' (which seems particularly odd, given how the heart is a dense, fibrous muscle).

No matter what happened to them in terms of their relationship, Carre Otis had a deep and profound effect on Rourke. He still describes her as 'my best friend', and stressed to me how he would never get over her. The pair still talk on the phone regularly, and are still there for one another when either is in need of the emotional support that only the other can provide.

But in 1998, Rourke was in a deep funk. The love of his life was gone. Professionally, he was sinking lower and lower with each passing year. Even the odd ray of hope had lately amounted to nothing more than a momentary triumph, before the inevitable step back. But the next step forward for Mickey Rourke would be an invitation to work on one of the most eagerly awaited American films for twenty years.

# Chapter Fourteen

# DON'T CALL IT A COMEBACK ...

**'I can take whatever you dish out, I'm twice the man you are.' – *Private Witt (Jim Caviezel)*, *The Thin Red Line***

*The Thin Red Line* marked the third film in 25 years from poetically gifted filmmaker Terence Malick. His first film, in 1975, was the brilliant *Badlands*, followed by the equally compelling *Days of Heaven* two years later. Then nothing was heard from Malick for decades. There had been rumours, but it wasn't until Twentieth Century Fox gave the green light to this ambitious World War II epic that anyone could be sure a new film from Malick was finally on the way. All of Hollywood was abuzz with the news. The notoriously reclusive Malick had chosen to adapt a dense, complex novel by war veteran James Jones (author of *From Here to Eternity*), about the epic battles in the South Pacific for control of Guadalcanal. It would be one of the finest war films ever committed to celluloid, possessed of an intense visual poetry.

The film would have over 70 speaking roles, not merely consisting of a few lines but over 70 distinct characters. Malick strove to cast each and every role with precise calculation, and he certainly had his pick of actors to aid him in his cause. Virtually every male actor in Hollywood was trying desperately to get in on the project. Malick would hold readings of his mammoth script (almost 200 pages long) with a roomful of A- and B-list actors, make some notes both mental and written, then hold another reading with a different set of A- and B-listers to see if anyone in this group stood head and shoulders above the other. Then he would have another reading with a mixed group from the first and second readings.

Leonardo DiCaprio badly wanted to be a part of the film, and actually invited Malick to hold one of the readings at his house. But, despite his obvious marquee value, and the fact that he has shown himself to be a pretty decent actor in the past, he was not selected. Mickey Rourke was chosen for a role, as a grunt who has seen too much action but wants to stay the course until the battle has been won, because he has nothing left to go home to – echoing where Rourke was in his own life on one level.

And while Malick certainly cast his film with a boatload of stars, he would also pick relative unknowns to fill very important roles as well. Sean Penn accepted the lead, but his co-star was a young actor named Jim Caviezel (who would go on to play Jesus in Aramaic in *The Passion of the Christ*). John Travolta took a small role (even though he felt unsuited for it), because he felt that he owed something to Malick – twenty years earlier, he had been first choice to play the lead in *Days of Heaven*, but dropped out at the last minute, thinking the film was too small for his career at the time. (Richard Gere inherited the role.) Canadian actor Elias Koteas (Rourke's co-star in *Desperate Hours*) is great as the humanitarian captain who always puts the lives and safety of his men first. Nick Nolte was cast as the West Point-trained veteran who is desperate to make his mark on the war, and delivered one of the best performances in his long career. Adrien Brody, Rourke's co-star in *Bullet* and a future Oscar winner for *The Pianist*, was cast in a major role, only to see it whittled down at the editing stage to a few brief glimpses. Which is exactly what happened to Mickey Rourke – in spades.

'I'm off to Borneo or some fucking place to do this war movie,' Rourke told a journalist for the now defunct *Bikini* magazine. 'I am told that this is a big movie and the script is really good, really good, so I hope this works out.' The location was actually in Australia, and Rourke would spend months filming his part, only to see the entire performance edited out. Still, he enjoyed working with the artistic, meticulous Terence Malick, and the fact that he was cast in the film, when so many other big-name talents had offered to work for Malick for nothing, was certainly a shot in the arm for his confidence. But the fact that his work was never to be seen was very disappointing – although similar experiences were shared by Viggo Mortensen, Gary Oldman, Bill Pullman and Lukas Haas. All made the first cut of the film, as did Rourke, but it was almost six hours long, whereas Malick was contracted to deliver three hours or less. Maybe one day a DVD director's cut of *The Thin Red Line* will be released, and we will be able to see Rourke's performance in the film, alongside the other aforementioned actors.

Rourke would head back home in pretty much the same position that he was in when he left – an actor who had been all but forgotten by mainstream Hollywood, remembered only for a bad reputation.

After returning home, Rourke took a few roles in films that showed fairly little promise. He was desperate for money, and had even considered taking construction jobs on the side. 'Yeah, it was a strange time,' said Rourke later. 'I called up a guy who used to hang with me and asked him if he knew where I might get some construction work and he just brushed me off and told me he didn't have time for my shit. That was a pretty hard lesson in itself.'

He did accept a trip to Ireland for a small role in a curious little film called *Shergar*. He plays a character named Gavin O'Rourke, in a story based on a true-life incident in which members of the IRA kidnapped a champion racehorse called Shergar, to ransom it for cash to support their cause. In the film, the plot is foiled by a young boy who stumbles on their hiding place and calls in the rescuers. Rourke plays only the smallest of roles, but took the job because he needed the money and was still very interested in films about the Irish situation.

He would follow this with a terrible movie called *Out in Fifty*, another low-budget indie film, written and directed by two Mickey Rourke fans, Bojesse Christopher and Scott Leet. This crime drama – once again from the post-Tarantino school of senseless violence masquerading as cool indie filmmaking – is about a reformed ex-con who gets manipulated into a love triangle and becomes a scapegoat in a revenge murder plot. Rourke plays a character named Jack Bracken and only appears sporadically, but you have to be a rabid Mickey Rourke fan to get anything out of this film at all. It was shot in Hollywood on an obvious shoestring budget, never made it to theatres and did next to no business in the home video market either.

Rourke's next film would be one of his least seen and least appreciated, but it is also one of the most interesting. *Shades* is a Belgian film, shot in Brussels and Antwerp. Rourke clearly saw it as another one to take just for the money, but he also took obvious delight in his character and was able to bring some ascerbic authenticity to it. While it can only be found, if it all, in the deepest reaches of video store bins, audiences in Belgium were appreciative. In Antwerp, a place with a vibrant art and fashion scene that seems to be one of the best kept cultural secrets in Europe, a young woman designer told me, 'It was wonderful to have a guy like Mickey Rourke here to make one of our films, it gave our film industry here a sense of international legitimacy. After all, he was a very big star.'

*Shades* is about a film being made in Belgium, a serial-killer-on-the-loose psychodrama based on the autobiography of an actual Belgian murderer serving life in prison. The film within a film is being directed by a bad-boy American director who has hit the skids in Hollywood, taking the job on a foreign film for the money and the slim chance that it might put him back on the map. The serial killer is being played by a prima donna American actor with discipline problems – not to mention drug and alcohol abuse problems – whose career hangs by a thread in Hollywood, and is looking to grab some attention with this flashy role. *Shades* takes us through the day to day rigours of holding a low-budget film together, from the point of view of a flashy producer with stars in his eyes, who still has to deal with daily financial woes and wild temperaments.

*Shades* was directed by one of the better directors in Belgium, Erik Van Looy, and there is a lot of material in the film that suggests it's a loosely fictionalised version of the life of another Belgian filmmaker, Guy Lee Thys – himself credited as one of the screenwriters.

Rourke is very good in this film. It almost appears like he's parodying the strange reputation that had attached itself to his name. Here is a celebrity director who enjoyed most of what fame once brought him, while at the same time he knows that his days of being an artist have waned and his days of being a hack for hire are here and now. You can see Rourke having fun with the role, taking little shots at some of the asshole directors he has worked with, while paying homage to some of the better ones, through his performance. He allows himself to look rumpled and worn out, with his long, stringy, greasy hair plastered down on his head and his cigarette strained voice, which jibes with a lot of the cheap shots that gossip columnists had been taking at him for years.

Rourke did his job in Belgium, collected his dough, then returned home to the dark uncertainty of a career that just wasn't going anywhere – not even slowly. He was slipping further and further into depression and despair.

It is not commonly known that Mickey Rourke is a devout Catholic. It seems that writing about it would conflict with the assertion that he is some kind of demonic force. But, in fact, he credits his Catholic faith with saving him at this time – not just saving his career, but actually saving his life.

Rourke is quite open about the fact that he speaks to his priest as often as he can. Father Pete, an old-time parish priest in New York, smokes a cigarette with him while hearing his confession. Rourke specifically credits Father Pete with talking him out of a very real intent to commit suicide. During this time, his depression and his complete loss of any feelings of self-worth led to him drinking to excess and seriously contemplating self-destruction. He checked himself into a psychiatric clinic for a weekend because he simply could not handle the anxiety a moment longer. 'If I wasn't a Catholic I would have blown my brains out,' said Rourke. 'I would pray to God, I would say, "Please God, send me down a ray of daylight."'

But this was also a time of home video and DVD proliferation that made an actor or director's entire career available for anyone to peruse or refer to. And there were a lot of actors who looked upon Mickey Rourke's earlier work as an inspiration, not swayed or influenced in the least by his reputation. Steve Buscemi was one such actor, and, through appearances in a string of high-profile films, was now positioned to direct films himself, and to be involved in the casting. Buscemi, the bug-eyed indie film darling who had become a favourite of the Coen brothers, had worked with Rourke a few years earlier on *The Last Outlaw*. He had already made a fairly well received film called *Trees Lounge*, and wanted to follow it up with something tougher and harder hitting. He came across the perfect material in the shape of a screenplay called *Animal Factory*, by writer/actor/ex-con Edward Bunker.

Buscemi had known Bunker ever since the two appeared together as actors in Tarantino's *Reservoir Dogs*, with Buscemi as Mr. Pink and Bunker as Mr. Blue. Bunker was also acquainted with another ex-con turned actor, a guy with one of the most frighteningly distinct tough-guy faces in all of moviedom, Danny Trejo (*Heat*, *Point Blank* with Rourke), and the two had been working on the script together, based on a novel by Bunker. The novel and screenplay are set in prison (where a lot of Bunker's prose is set, including part of his first novel – the minor masterpiece *No Beast So Fierce*, which became the film *Straight Time* starring Dustin Hoffman). The story concerns a young man incarcerated in a rundown prison for a two-year term. This kid, Ron Decker (Edward Furlong), is terrified of what awaits him. That fear is intensified when one of the first things he witnesses in prison is a violent uprising. He is then taken under the wing of a long-term con named Earl Copen (Willem Dafoe), who has found a way to work every angle of prison life to his advantage. With the weight of Copen behind him, Decker finds a little respect among the violent prison gangs and goonish guards. But life, as he finds out, is never easy in prison, even for those with a bit of weight behind them. In this place everything is about day to day survival.

Buscemi read the novel and liked it even more than the screenplay. He agreed to make the film, but wanted more of the depth of the novel applied to the script, which Bunker managed to work in easily.

Then Buscemi called Mickey Rourke and offered him a role in the film. There would be no need for an audition or a reading, as he knew what Rourke had. But the role that Buscemi had in mind was one that Rourke was not sure he was ready for. Still, he needed the work, and besides – he was an actor. Buscemi wanted him to play an inmate transvestite called Jan the Actress.

'When he told me that I thought he was fucking playing with me,' said Rourke. 'I tried to explain to him that I could not be further away from what I thought a transvestite looked like, but Steve had something in mind, so I went with it.' He decided to throw himself into the role and not only give Buscemi what he wanted, but add a few dimensions of his own. He decided to get into the character right away by starting with the costume he/she would wear.

'I went around Los Angeles for awhile before shooting the film and checked out some lingerie shops,' said Rourke. 'I'd be trying on bras and shit and people were looking at me, I knew they were recognising me. I don't give a shit about that stuff but when I start getting calls from my mother and she tells me she has been reading about where I have been hanging out in the tabloids and have to explain it to her – that part is a fucking drag.'

Rourke also visited a Los Angeles beauty parlour to have his nails done. He tells a funny story of putting on flamboyant women's clothing, women's shoes and a wig, and heading to the airport, bound for the location. He had had his dentist remove his two false front teeth, his original teeth having been lost years previously during his early days as a boxer. (He was never shy about revealing this. Once, in a Los Angeles restaurant/bar, he found himself sharing drinks with members of the Calgary Flames hockey team. They all had a great time removing their various false teeth and bridgework, and plunking it all down on the table.) He actually frightened a few small children on the plane, who could not figure out who, or what, this person was. When he finally arrived on the set no one recognised him. Even Buscemi, who gave the directive that he should appear in drag, had to be convinced that this crazy looking dude was actually Mickey Rourke.

And it wasn't all about his appearance. Rourke actually worked very hard to create a backstory for his character, even though he/she would appear in the film only briefly. 'I played her like a person who had been in the prison system since she was a teenager and knew nothing else but prison life,' he said. 'I had a bit of an advantage here because when I first came out to California I worked as a bouncer in a transvestite club – I saw all these guys and sometimes I actually had to remind myself that they were actually men. They think of themselves as women but they really aren't.'

Buscemi admitted that Rourke was not his first choice for Jan the Actress, but once the idea was in his head he had to follow through. Once Rourke got on the set he just blew everyone away. 'He did his own nails, he did his own hair, he brought his own wardrobe,' said Buscemi. 'Mickey even wrote his own monologue – the part about Jan turning into a butterfly and flying between the bars and all that stuff, that was all Mickey.'

Buscemi would go on to say of working with Rourke, 'I had Mickey on the set for just a day and a half but when we were shooting with him I just didn't want it to end. I didn't want to stop rolling because he was just so fascinating to watch.'

Filmed in Philadelphia, in a decommissioned prison, *Animal Factory* is an effective look at the dehumanisation and demoralisation of prison life. Rourke is a standout in his brief appearance, with some fine work also by Willem Dafoe and a creepy turn from Tom Arnold. It previewed on 20 January 2000, at the Sundance Film Festival, to very enthusiastic responses. It wouldn't make it to a lot of North American screens, although it did moderately well in overseas markets, and was sold to cable TV where it was first shown in July 2000.

After Rourke completed his extended cameo role, it was back to the treadmill. Back to praying for that ray of daylight.

In less than a month, a beam of light would cut across Rourke's path by courtesy of a fellow brawler – Sylvester Stallone. Stallone had once said of Rourke, 'Mickey has the heart and soul of a character actor but the body and image of a leading man.' Rourke would echo the positive sentiments, completing the mutual admiration society. 'Good old Sly,' he said. 'I should have lis-

*As villain Cyrus Paice, with Sylvester Stallone in* Get Carter *(2000). This remake of a British classic was badly received, but Rourke was grateful to be in a big-budget film.*

tened to him ten years ago when he was telling me that I should conduct my acting career like a business. He has done a great job at that. Plus, people have to remember that Sly is actually a great actor. I should have listened to him.'

By this time, in 2000, Stallone's career had also seen better days. But he was linked with producer Elie Samaha, who had produced *Animal Factory* and won some fat backing from overseas banks to fund films through his company, Franchise Pictures. It was Franchise who were keeping Stallone in starring roles. Their films were put together with a lot of chequered financing from a lot of different sources, then offered up to a major studio for distribution, in most cases Warner Bros. The list of producers on Samaha and Stallone's latest film, *Get Carter*, would number no fewer than fifteen! But the bottom line is that the films got made and received wide releases.

*Get Carter* is based on the 1971 film of the same title that starred Michael Caine (who plays a small role in the remake), and concerns a paid thug named Jack who breaks bones for the Mob. He returns to his native Seattle to attend the funeral of his brother, who has died under

**119**

mysterious circumstances. Jack does his own investigating and sets about ensuring that every-one involved in his brother's death pays for it, the Jack Carter way.

Despite the mockery he has taken during the latter part of his career, Sylvester Stallone is not a stupid man. On the contrary, he is a well read, witty, interesting man. But, since becoming a legitimate Hollywood legend with his *Rocky* series, Stallone had allowed himself to slip into a place where ego and self-absorption took complete control, resulting in some seriously dubious career choices.

With *Get Carter*, Stallone attempted to make a *film noir* (which was how he described his earlier film *Cobra*, though that was a laughable assertion) and wanted it to be as stylish as pos-sible. Director Stephen Kay provided an abundance of style, but also infused the film with an awful lot of senseless violence. The casting was solid, with Scottish actor Alan Cumming play-ing the dot.com billionaire brat peripherally involved in the murder, and Mickey Rourke as Cyrus Paice, a shady club owner directly involved in the murder, but unafraid of Jack Carter – because he is just as big a bruiser as Carter is.

*Get Carter* is not a particularly bad film, and is actually quite visually stylish. However, it's another of that endless string of contemporary films that look and feel more like music videos. It has some terrible dialogue – 'My name is Jack Carter, and you don't want to know me.' – and is further hampered by nonexistent character development. A lot of the film's criticism was aimed at Stallone himself, because he had been perceived over the years, not always fairly, as on a downward spiral of self-parody.

But from Rourke's perspective, this film represented something he needed very badly – a well-placed friend willing to extend a hand to him.

*Get Carter* was shot on location in Las Vegas, Seattle, Washington and Vancouver, British Columbia, on a $40 million budget. It was released on 25 September 2000, in New York, and 4 October in Los Angeles, but only managed to pull in about $15 million at the domestic box office. It didn't do much better in the foreign markets either.

But ask Mickey Rourke, and he will tell you that the comeback he had been trying to achieve for so long began with *Get Carter*. 'I still had some other small stuff that I had agreed to do for the work, but it was that one [*Get Carter*] that cracked the ice. I started getting some interesting calls and I started to feel that there might actually be some fucking hope.'

But there was still the small stuff to do, so he remained optimistic but cautious.

Rourke had never been much into sci-fi or horror, but one of his rare forays into genre film came just after *Get Carter* with a small role in *They Crawl* – a kind of throwback to the sci-fi films of the 1950s. Governmental research into genetic engineering has produced huge killer cock-roaches that will eventually replace the more conventional weapons of mass destruction. The government plans to use these cockroaches to carpet bomb an enemy, devouring his soldiers and decimating his country without a shot being fired. The film was directed by John Allardice, a veteran of several *Star Trek* TV episodes. He cast Rourke because, as was typical by now, he was a fan and wanted him in his film even if just for a few minutes. The largely unknown leads (Daniel Cosgrove and Tamara Davies) deliver standard perfunctory horror movie performances, but there's also a quirky little turn by legendary rapper Tone Loc.

This is a strange little film, and Rourke's performance is even stranger. Manic and weird, it constitutes one of the very few appearances by Mickey Rourke that is actually embarassing.

This little piece of nothing was followed by one of the most truly compelling films Rourke has done in years. It happened because director Sean Penn was looking for the most intense actors he could find for his rivetingly dark film, *The Pledge*. Jack Nicholson stars as a retiring Nevada lawman, Jerry Black, who pledges to a young mother that he will – if it is the last thing he ever does – solve the mystery surrounding the murder of her little girl. There have been other cases of missing or murdered girls in the area fitting the same general modus operandi, leading Jerry to believe that the man languishing in jail is not responsible for the murder at all. The ex-lawman even buys a gas station in the region of the murders so that he can maintain his hands-on investigation. Then he befriends a young woman (Robin Wright Penn) with a young blonde daughter who is exactly the same physical type as the murdered girls, as his obsessive search for the person responsible grows ever deeper and more urgent.

As is the case with the other films directed by Penn (*The Indian Runner*, *The Crossing Guard*), *The Pledge* is dark, intense, extremely well acted, and directed with a remarkably sure hand. The cast is also uniformly good: from Nicholson, who is always solid, through Robin Wright (Penn's wife), Benicio Del Toro, Harry Dean Stanton, Helen Mirren, Sam Sheppard and Aaron Eckhardt.

Rourke is heart-wrenchingly brilliant in his one scene in the film. It is an emotionally charged scene in which he plays Brian Olstad, a father who describes losing his child to an act of violence. Rourke's few moments are as memorable as any others in the whole running time of the film.

Rourke moved from this tiny role into a role in a small film, part of a series of shorts by some of the most revered directors in world cinema. Rourke's contribution was a segment with a running time of just eight minutes, directed by the artistically accomplished Wong Kar Wai (*Chungking Express*), produced by David Fincher (director of *Se7en* and *Fight Club)* and written by Andrew Kevin Walker (*Se7en*, *The Legend of Sleepy Hollow*). The idea behind these films was either boldly ingenious or utterly insidious, depending on your point of view. They were made as advertisements for BMW cars, after the marketing crew at BMW came up with the idea to hire four top-flight directors to make four short films with major actors, all based around a cool Driver (Clive Owen) who drives people around, gets chased, and generally just looks great behind the wheel of a BMW. Rourke's sequence was called *The Hire: The Follow*, and like the others was only available on the Internet. He is featured as the Husband, who is following his Wife (Adrianna Lima) and being tailed by the Employer (Forest Whitaker). It was slick PR.

I asked Clive Owen about the films. 'I was originally resistant to the idea,' said Owen. 'But then I started to look closely at who they had locked into the project, people like [director] John Frankenheimer and Wong Kar Wai and Mickey Rourke and Madonna, and what they had in mind, and I then could not come up with any valid reasons why I would *not* want to do this.'

I first saw these films on a computer display, set up in a tent by BMW at the 2001 Cannes International Film Festival. I was struck by how well made they were, considering their limited purpose. More importantly, they showed that Mickey Rourke was once again working with top-drawer talent. He was still around, and he still had it.

# Chapter Fifteen
# MICKEY NORTH

**'. . . because he is Mickey Fucking Rourke!' –
Filmmaker Bruce McDonald, on why he cast Mickey
Rourke in his film Picture Claire.**

'Could someone please get me a blanket or a coat or something?' croaked Mickey Rourke, on the set of a Canadian neo-*noir* shot in a rundown section of Toronto called the Kensington Market. When no blanket appeared, we started to scavenge around the set for one. The closest we came was a hooded fleece sweatshirt left on the back of a chair. (By its size and scent, we deduced it had been left there by a female crew member.) It was good enough for Mickey, even though this was a late February night in Toronto – one of the cruellest, ugliest months, when snow on the ground is no longer white or even off-white, but a greyish black. The air was cold and raw, not crisp but damp, chilling us down to the bone all night long. But on this night Mickey Rourke was walking around in jeans, a sleeveless T-shirt and a wool toque over his long, dyed blonde hair. The sweatshirt was for his Chihuahua that he cradled protectively in his arms, a pet he was never without for long during the course of the shoot.

Rourke is remarkably gentle around these little animals. With names like Bo-Jacks and Loki, he has grown to love these pets, and their siblings and descendants, so profoundly that they have a soothing psychological effect on him. However, the opposite is true should anyone mess with his dogs. On a flight around this time, Rourke got quite hostile towards a flight attendant who kicked Loki's carrying case, trying to move the item under his seat without realising it contained his dog. 'Fuck you bitch, that's my fucking dog you're kicking there!' is how Mickey remembers his response. Rourke is quick to confess that caring for these little animals gave him a renewed sense of responsibility, a reason to think of something other than himself at a time when he was lost, and swirling downward at an ever increasing rate.

Rourke was contracted to shoot his role in *Picture Claire* in just four days, and was in Toronto for only five days. The writer-director of the film is one of the most eclectically talented to be found in the Canadian cinema, an industry woefully lacking in self-esteem. Bruce McDonald has made some interesting films in his time – like *Dance Me Outside*, produced by Lifetime Achievement Academy Award winner Norman Jewison, for whom McDonald once worked as a driver – but the film that grabbed Rourke's attention is called *Hard Core Logo.* It's a mock documentary about the last cross-country tour of a fading punk band. Shot with energy and authenticity, it gained the attention of Quentin Tarantino, who agreed to release it on home video through his Rolling Thunder distribution company.

'I had never heard of Bruce McDonald,' said Rourke. 'Not that that says anything about him, I don't follow the movie business that closely. But then this script arrives called *Claire's Hat*, I believe it was called [an alternative title considered early on by McDonald], and it was packaged up with a copy of a movie called *Hard Core Logo*. I watched that film and I just fucking loved it. At first I thought it was a real documentary about a real grimy little punk band. When I was told that it was a feature that was written and directed by this guy McDonald, I was pretty excited about working with this fucking guy. Even though I was doing what amounted to a walk on . . . I really needed the fucking money at the time.'

*Picture Claire* was conceived as a *film noir*, the kind of film McDonald loves. 'I grew up digging movies like *Double Indemnity* and Melville's *Le Samourai*,' he said. 'I always wanted to write my own cool as fuck thriller, shoot it right in my back yard and cast people I dug, not the people that the money guys were shoving down my throat, but cool people. I didn't care if they were from Canada or Hollywood or Brussels or Reykjavik or wherever.'

The story of the film concerns a French-Canadian girl (a woefully miscast Juliette Lewis) from Montreal, who travels to Toronto after being burned out of her apartment. She is heading to the home of a photographer she had a brief affair with, who once invited her to stay with him in Toronto, believing she would never take him up on the offer. Upon her arrival, the film becomes a wrong-place-at-the-wrong-time crime drama, involving a couple of sleazeball underworld types, crooked cops, crooked customs agents, missing money and stashed diamonds. And while this all sounds a bit rehashed (there really is no such thing as a truly original mystery film plot), McDonald attempted to take those tried and tested *noir* characters and stamp them with his own imprint.

Casting was crucial. But Juliette Lewis, a fine actress in films like *Cape Fear* and *Kalifornia*, was the wrong choice to play a French-Canadian who can barely speak English. Her accent is atrociously bad and clichéd, so much so that it's a distraction. Rourke was well cast as a mysterious, double-crossing thug named Eddie, and that exceedingly good bad girl Gina Gershon plays his contact/mule, an amoral woman who is after nothing but a quick score. Canadian actor Callum Keith Rennie is terrific in his role as Laramie, a strange character who can never be pegged as a good guy or a bad guy. Rennie is probably the closest thing that Canada has produced to James Dean, something that was said about Mickey Rourke back in the day. (But Rourke was in a place where he could run with that hype. Rennie, as a Canadian, hasn't anywhere to run with it.)

Rourke's role is of the blink-and-you'll-miss-him variety. I asked McDonald about that and he smiled uncomfortably. 'I cast him because he is Mickey Fucking Rourke,' he said. 'And I have always, always wanted to work with him. Everybody else seems to have forgotten about the guy or bought into all the bullshit said about him – but I wanted him in this film bad. I wrote the character while fantasising about actually getting Mickey Rourke to play the character.' That being the case, why then did McDonald not write him a bigger, juicier part? 'Yeah man, I wanted to do that and I would have done that in a perfect world,' said McDonald. 'But there was a money issue involved. This was a low-budget movie [$4.5 million Canadian dollars] and I had a lot of speaking roles and a lot of night shoots . . .'

Rourke plays his character effectively, but that isn't saying much. He is asked to growl and say his lines with a monotone malevolence, while cuddling Gina Gershon in a diner. He looks suitably rough around the edges, but the fact that he shows up in just two scenes has 'gimmick casting' written all over it. And that's too bad, because McDonald wanted a lot more from the role and Rourke deserved a lot more from it.

I observed how the director fought the urge towards hero-worship when Rourke was on the set, and asked him about it during a quiet moment when the set was being re-dressed. 'You have to understand that when I was growing up, Mickey Rourke was the man, the icon of cool,' said McDonald. 'McQueen was slightly before my time, as was Mitchum. But Rourke was the guy you wanted to be like. Guys wanted to be him and women wanted to fuck him . . . underneath it all was a really good actor with a shitload of natural instincts and sensitivities.'

During a couple of takes, Rourke appeared to be having trouble with his lines. Director McDonald quietly said, 'Cut.' After a couple of these stop-and-starts, Rourke quietly called him over and whispered something to him. The next three takes were shot and printed. A while later, in a trailer over some coffee, I asked Rourke what he whispered to McDonald. 'I just told him that I was trying it out all these different ways and trying different line readings, and by cutting the scenes prematurely he probably wrecked a couple of cool fucking moments,' said Rourke. 'I told him to trust me and to roll with me.'

During his stay in Toronto, Rourke made good use of his time off. He was often seen enjoying himself at jazzy clubs like the Reservoir Lounge on Wellington Street, or the Avenue Bar of the Toronto Four Seasons Hotel. Rourke was staying a few blocks south of the Four Seasons, at a charming, newly renovated boutique hotel called the Windsor Arms that once, in a previous incarnation, used to boast Elizabeth Taylor and Richard Burton as frequent guests in a perpetually booked suite.

Karen Poppell, the PR boss at the Windsor Arms at the time, remembered Rourke as a courteous and soft-spoken man. 'He would often come into the lounge for a bite to eat or a drink,' she said. 'The first time he came into the lounge he brought his little dog with him. I had to explain to him that Health Canada would not permit the dog to be in a commercial place where people ate. So from then on he would simply leave his little dog with one of the doormen to watch while he was in the lounge.'

I asked Ms Poppell if Rourke's reputation as a hell-raiser was born out at any time during his stay. 'Not once,' she answered. 'In fact the only time he ever asked me for anything out of the ordinary was when he asked me to sit with him at his table and help him learn his lines.'

Things went bad for *Picture Claire* after the shooting was completed. The film was initially deemed unreleasable by the company financing it, Alliance Atlantis, who completely abandoned it without a theatrical release. Bruce McDonald was furious. 'Fucking Alliance Atlantis, man, fucking Robert Lantos [the wannabe mogul who greenlit the film] was always on the set telling me how much he was digging the footage that he saw,' said McDonald. 'Then when a couple of these pasty-faced asshole critics started ragging on a very early cut of the film, Lantos panicked and copped out on me.' McDonald was planning to make another film, a kind of 'un-making of' documentary on what happened to him and his movie, but was warned by the Alliance Atlantic legal department that, if he were to show a frame of footage from *their* film, he would be sued to substantial effect.

*Picture Claire* was actually scheduled to play the Toronto International Film Festival. About five minutes into the running time, the lights came up and a festival staff person stepped onto the stage and announced, 'Due to events happening in New York City, all screenings have been cancelled.' This was the morning of 11 September 2001. I was able to see the film just over a month later at the tiny northern Sudbury Films Festival. Bruce McDonald was in attendance and took the stage for a brief Q and A after the film. He was a little

*Mickey north of the border, with his biker buddy Carl from the Downtown Toronto Hells Angels.*

drunk and looked grungy in his cowboy hat and torn jeans. He was sheepish because, by this time, the film has already been all but written off. One earnest young cineaste stood up and asked who the cool guy in the sunglasses was in the diner scene. McDonald shook his head and smiled, while almost imperceptibly saying, 'Man, that was Mickey Fucking Rourke.'

As the ice was breaking for Rourke, the spectre of his old reputation was still haunting him. He was up for a lead role in a film called *In the Cut*, that was to co-star Nicole Kidman. (It eventually starred Meg Ryan and Mark Ruffalo in the leads.) But Ms Kidman decided she was not about to co-star in a film with Mickey Rourke, and vetoed him. Because she had casting approval her decision had to be respected. Rourke was obviously disappointed, and a bit angered, by this turn of events. 'I can't understand that shit,' he said. 'I mean, she has never even met me. Why would she discount me without even having met me?'

One of the more positive events that happened during this time was the securing of a new, young agent. David Unger told Rourke that he would take him on as a client, only on the conditions that Rourke follow his instructions to the letter and behave himself whenever Unger got him a gig. 'I am really indebted to David Unger,' said Rourke. 'He is not a yes-man, he is not the kind of asshole that I was used to having around me.'

One of the jobs that Unger urged Rourke to take was a crazy little low-budget film called *Spun*, to be directed by Swedish whizz-kid music video director Jonas Akerlund. Rourke was initially resistant to the idea. He didn't like the script, didn't like the character he was being asked to play, and particularly didn't like the low-ball fee he was offered. But Unger was adamant and insistent, reminding Rourke of the terms of their agreement. He felt that it could be a hot little film at places like the Sundance Festival, gaining the kind of attention that Unger was seeking for his new client.

'I really didn't have too much interest in this piece at first,' said Rourke. 'But part of my deal with my new agent was that I took the things that he said I should take and that I was to trust his judgement. I really did put my career in his hands because he went out on something of a limb by taking me on – so I took his word for it and did the movie.'

Rourke's initial resistance stemmed from how the script felt like a lot of the other stuff he had been doing just for the money. Akerlund had made some fantastic, high-energy videos for the likes of Moby, U2 and The Prodigy, but was an untested feature filmmaker. The film was clearly designed in such a way as to show his visual virtuosity on the big screen. The screenplay, by Will Del Los Santos and Creighton Vero, was based on hundreds of interviews with real drug dealers and 'tweekers' (methamphetamine addicts), so the dialogue was completely authentic. There was originally a plan to use this material for the purposes of a documentary called *The Cook* (the character ultimately played by Rourke in the film), which was to be more about how the stuff is made and distributed by street chemists. But Akerlund decided he could finesse the story and the visuals, and make a lot more impact with a feature film.

The story is a simple one. A middle-class tweeker (played with gusto by the terrific young actor Jason Schwartzman) has allowed his addiction to get out of control. He is introduced to the guy who actually manufactures the meth, The Cook (Rourke), and his lower level dealer (played with wide-eyed glee by John Leguizamo). What follows is a three-day orgy of drug abuse and craziness. One interesting point of casting is that of The Man, an effete drug user with money, played by Eric Roberts. It allowed Roberts and Rourke to play their first couple of scenes together since *The Pope of Greenwich Village*.

(Rourke was asked to be in a film about counterfeiting a year previously, called *The Luck of the Draw*, alongside Michael Madsen, Ice-T, Dennis Hopper and Roberts. But he dropped out at the last moment, it was said, because the director, Luca Bercovici, refused to allowed his Chihuahua to take part in his scenes – in other words, Rourke supposedly refused the role because the director wouldn't write his dog into the script. The other side of the story was that Mickey simply became unavailable for the film because of his schedules.)

Shooting in rough sections of downtown Los Angeles and North Hollywood went as smoothly as could be expected, considering the wildness of the story and the characters. 'I got along well with Jonas,' said Rourke. 'I liked what he was doing, I liked his approach to the work, approaching it like he was some kind of new age painter using film to make this abstract painting that was reflecting the times we live in.'

It's an astute analogy when you consider how the film was made. It was shot in a scant 22 days, and when Akerlund turned in his first cut it came in at a deliriously paced three hours. As it stands, the 101-minute theatrical print holds the record for the most cuts ever made in a feature film, at over 5000.

*Spun* is frantic, seeming to race through its running time at about five times the normal speed. The performances are uniformly good, and you never doubt for a second that these are drug-crazed maniacs who have lost all semblance of control over their lives. When it arrives at its closing credits, you actually feel drained at having sat through such a manically paced film.

For Mickey Rourke, the film represented another positive step on his journey back to respectability, though it was a far cry from being a hit. Made for a budget of just under $3 million, it grossed only about half that during its theatrical run. It was redeemed somewhat on home video, but not enough for the movie to be considered successful. But *Spun* did make it into a number of film festivals around the world: from Toronto to Gijon, from the Paris Nemo Festival to the Copenhagen International Film Festival.

Rourke was suddenly on the world cinema stage again, and proved that he could still attract positive attention. When the film was shown at Sundance, he went along to promote it. Daryl Hannah was also there, promoting her latest film, and the pair would be seen around Park City together during the festival. It was written that they were a couple, and were seen 'all over each other'. But there was really nothing to it. They were just two old friends, enjoying each other's company for the first time since working together on *The Pope of Greenwich Village*. (Hannah had played Rourke's leggy WASP girlfriend but seemed oddly out of place in that film.)

Rourke would lend himself to one more small film before things shifted into a higher gear. He wasn't alone. There were a lot of actors who lined up to be in *Masked and Anonymous* at drastically reduced fees – names like Jeff Bridges, Val Kilmer, Christian Slater, Ed Harris, Penelope Cruz, and Jessica Lange. And they all did so because of who was starring in the film and had co-written the screenplay – Bob Dylan. Larry Charles, known for his work in TV comedy as a writer on *Mad About You* and *Seinfeld*, co-wrote and directed the film under the pen name Rene Fontaine, while Dylan used Sergei Petrov for his screenwriting credit.

*Masked and Anonymous* is a surreal political comedy about a United States on the brink of widespread social revolution. Two greed-ridden producers named Uncle Sweetheart (John Goodman) and Nina Veronica (Jessica Lange) are trying to organise a massive benefit concert, but need the participation of a legendary singer named Jack Fate (Dylan) – who is actually in jail at the time. But Fate is mysteriously released from prison so that he can perform, as rock journalist Tom Friend (Jeff Bridges) starts to look at what's going on behind the concert, which goes ahead as planned just as the revolution explodes. Rourke shows up in a couple of scenes as a character named Edmund, who seems to be a politician, but the movie is so vague and pointless that it's hard to determine exactly what his role is.

Bob Dylan is a terrible actor, wooden and emotionless, and the entire movie is just one big, self-indulgent ego-stroke. While *Masked and Anonymous* did get a theatrical release, it bombed in a big way. (Listings indicate that on the week of 14 December 2003 the film grossed a grand total of $638.)

But all was not for naught in 2003. Rourke was about to be cast in a film by a director he would really click with, and who would eventually bring him back into the big time. Robert Rodriguez's ode to Sergio Leone, *Once Upon a Time in Mexico*, came from an idea by his occasional collaborator Quentin Tarantino. He thought it would be cool if Rodriguez followed up *El Mariachi* and *Desperado* with a third film on a more epic scale, the way that Leone followed *A Fistful of Dollars* and *For a Few Dollars More* with *The Good, the Bad and the Ugly.* The plan was to start filming in 2001, but that was delayed by over a year (fortuitously for Rourke).

Rodriguez has become a wildly successful filmmaker despite his estrangement from Hollywood. It isn't that he hates Hollywood – it's just that he loves his hometown of Austin, Texas more. He has set up his own full service studio where he writes, shoots, produces, edits and even scores his films. The plan was to shoot *Once Upon a Time in Mexico* on high-definition video on a very tight schedule, and to experiment as much as he could using the ultra-cheap format.

Tarantino and Rodriguez are both huge fans of Mickey Rourke. Their idea of casting him in the role of Billy Chambers was also endorsed by another high-profile addition to the cast, Johnny Depp. Depp has been a long-time friend of Rourke's, and had once publicly proclaimed that *The Pope of Greenwich Village* is 'perfect cinema'. He was one of those friends who stuck with Rourke through the down times, and was even known to throw him birthday parties if the two were both in town.

I asked Mickey about his friendship with Depp. The mention of his name instantly produced a big smile and a shake of the head. 'Johnny is a great guy,' he said. 'And he has it down right, he knows how to play the game. He does his thing, he does the stuff that is expected of him, and then he gets the fuck out and goes to his family. He's a smart guy.'

Depp was only on the Mexican location for nine days and pretty much improvised all his dialogue (the screenplay was only 45 pages long to begin with), and is even credited with composing his character's theme music.

With the exception of the returning *Desperado* cast members like Antonio Banderas as El Mariachi, the guitar-playing gunman, and Selma Hayek as Carolina, most of the cast was filled out with actors who were fifth or sixth choice. Even the role of Sands (Depp) was first offered to George Clooney, then to Sean Penn, Nic Cage and Kurt Russell, before Depp agreed to do the film. Other cast members included Willem Dafoe, Ruben Blades, Eva Mendes and Enrique Iglesias.

The story is much like those found in spaghetti westerns, in that it involves a dangerous lone character (Banderas) who has been wronged in the past and now chooses to live a solitary life as a wanderer. He unwittingly becomes involved in an international plot involving the Mexican government, which has declared war on a drug cartel. The cartel boss (Dafoe) tries to get even by arranging for a coup to be staged against the president. Sands (Depp), a crazy CIA agent who wears a T-shirt identifying him as such, tries to short circuit the coup and get the cartel boss at the same time, enlisting the help of the mysterious guitar player/fighter El Mariachi.

It's a well-directed movie, possessing a tongue-in-cheek, off-the-wall quality that's refreshing in these days of pre-packaged, demographic-conscious studio junk. Johnny Depp performs outright cinematic larceny, stealing every scene he is in, while Mickey Rourke plays a character hiding out from American justice and working for the Barillo (Dafoe) cartel. He wears purple suits and a cowboy hat, and is never without his little Chihuahua – which, incidentally, ends up play-

*As a member of the drug cartel headed by Willem Dafoe (right) in* Once Upon a Time in Mexico *(2003).*
*Robert Rodriguez was indulgent enough to cast one of Rourke's beloved Chihuahuas.*

ing a significant role in the film. In keeping with the quirkiness, when Rourke's character is shot in the back it is all digitally drawn in. He was upset that the special effects squibs might damage the cool purple jacket he wanted to keep.

*Once Upon a Time in Mexico* is a very entertaining little diversion. It was a huge hit when it debuted in theatres in September 2003, making $23 million during its opening weekend (at an estimated cost of $29 million) and pulling in over $60 million in the domestic market and another $30 million or so from overseas, before making another killing on DVD.

*Once Upon a Time in Mexico* provided Rourke with exactly what he needed, even though his role in it was small. He was now aligned with a director he loved working with, and was part of the cast of a bona fide hit film.

But Mickey Rourke was not yet on easy street. In fact, he knew that he would never go back to where he previously was. But still, by now he had at least earned the right to work on worthwhile projects.

**129**

# Chapter Sixteen

# THE LAST CHANCE

**'This is the old days, this is the bad days, this is the all or nothing days.' – *Marv (Mickey Rourke), Sin City***

On 6 October 2004, Joey Rourke, Mickey's beloved half-brother, lost his long and valiant battle with numerous forms of cancer. (It was lung cancer that claimed his life.) Joey was as close to Mickey as anyone in the world. He was a fellow motorcycle enthusiast, and a rough and ready guy just like his brother. Mickey had spent the last twenty years doing whatever was in his power to assist his brother. No matter how much money he had, or didn't have, at a particular time, whatever he had was available to aid Joey's comfort and well being. Medical bills were paid. Private hospital rooms were arranged. At certain times it appeared that progress was being made. Joey did go into remission a number of times – only to be disheartened, when the heartless bastard that is cancer returned to terrorise him again.

Mickey would include his brother in his film projects whenever Joey was able to participate. Joey had small parts in *Johnny Handsome*, *Bullet* and *The Last Outlaw*, and served as Mickey's stand-in during the shooting of *Wild Orchid*.

Mickey's reaction to his brother's death was profoundly introspective and reflective. As he told his friend, the painter/filmmaker Julian Schnabel, 'There is no lying in my life now because of that [Joey's death]. That changes you greatly. Joe left me with tremendous strength because of something he said as the life was going out of him. He looked at me and said, "Hey bro, you've changed. I never thought you would. I thought you were always going to be crazy, but you've changed." And it meant a lot to him to see me change. So I am not going to fail again because I have worked very hard to understand that it is not only important to me to keep moving forward, but also because Joe wouldn't want me to fail.'

Rourke did indeed move forward. He accepted a voice-only role on a video game called *Driv3r*, which was an easy but lucrative gig. Rourke's character is a mean dude called Jericho. The story concerns two Miami cops who must traverse not only their hometown but Nice, and then Istanbul, on the trail of some car thieves, to prevent them from stealing the 40 most exotic cars in the world. The cops are voiced by tough-guy actors Ving Rhames and Michael Madsen, with the voice of punk rock legend Iggy Pop also turning up. A year later, Rourke would take up this lucrative sideline again when he agreed to be heard in the video game *True Crime: New*

*York City* – another violent tough-guy game for vidiots and computer geeks, with another host of cool actors: Christopher Walken, Laurence Fishburne, Mariska Hargitay and ex-porn star Traci Lords, alongside Rourke.

While working on *Driv3r*, Rourke received a call from a filmmaker which added to the positive momentum that had been developing. The fits and starts were now over; the opportunity to put his career right was now upon him. It was his chance to run with it or blow it.

*Man on Fire* is a remake (of sorts) of a 1987 film starring Scott Glenn. The screenplay for the 2004 version had actually been kicking around in various stages of development for a number of years.

Both films originate from the taut, suspenseful novel by A. J. Quinell, about a burned-out American government agent far from home, who is hired to protect the daughter of a rich family from kidnapping. But while both films carry the same basic plotline, they are miles apart in terms of the finished product.

Director Tony Scott's films have always been criticised for style over substance. For the most part that has been true, but there is nothing inherently wrong with it. His first feature, *The Hunger*, was all style but it worked. With his version of *Man on Fire*, he would tell an interesting story about how Mexican society is almost completely overwhelmed by crime and corruption, while seeming to function normally on the surface. Kidnapping is the number one growth industry in Mexico City, with the hiring of expensive bodyguards and private security teams being the second biggest.

Ironically, back in the 1980s, when the film had first gone into development, Scott expressed interest but was considered too inexperienced and lacking in a commercial track record. Much later, it went to Michael Bay, who turned it down flat (probably because it had too much in the way of story and character development for his taste). The project languished until it was thought that it might make a vehicle for a new young action filmmaker named Antoine Fuqua (*The Replacement Killers, Training Day*). Fuqua would have no doubt made an interesting version, but was already up to his neck in a huge budget film called *King Arthur*. The script then wound up back on the desk of . . . Tony Scott.

Scott, in the intervening years, had become the very personification of the commercial minded filmmaker in Hollywood, and easily passed the litmus test this time around. But back in the 1980s, the rights had reverted back to the author, who then sold them to producer Arnon Milchan, who made the 1987 version with Scott Glenn in the lead. (In this version the action is set in Europe, and the film was shot in Italy.) While both the 1987 version and Scott's version are based on the same book, they are very different interpretations and, other than the title, bear only the slightest resemblance to one another.

In the late 1980s, screenwriter Brian Helgelund had been browsing a video store. An enthusiastically geeky clerk behind the counter suggested he check out the '87 version of *Man on Fire*. Helgelund watched the film and loved it. (The video geek in the store was none other than Quentin Tarantino.) He sought out the novel and became determined to write a new screenplay, with the intention of pitching it with himself as director. But when Tony Scott's current project suddenly fell apart, he was freed up to direct *Man on Fire*. leaving Helgelund with just the writing credit. Robert De Niro was offered the lead role of Creasy, and would have been terrific, but could not commit. Then it was offered to Will Smith, for some bizarre reason, and Bruce Willis, who would have been even worse. Then one day, when Denzel Washington was visiting his doctor, he ran into Tony Scott awaiting a physical check-up. When the subject of *Man on Fire* came up, Washington was intrigued by Scott's description of the burned-out Creasy.

Christopher Walken was originally offered the role of Jordan, the role that Mickey Rourke would end up playing. But Walken had played a couple of characters like Jordan before, and said that the character of Rayburn interested him more, suggesting his friend Rourke for Jordan. And that was that.

Except that it wasn't quite as simple as that. Once again, there was some resistance from above against casting Mickey Rourke, despite the fact that the role was relatively small. But Scott had met with Rourke, knew his work, and was comfortable that he would be good in the role, and might even make some interesting contributions that weren't on the page. He fought for Rourke to be cast and finally won out. His loyalty to Rourke (and vice versa) would become another important building block in the actor's resurrection.

Once again, Rourke made the absolute most of his role, playing a seedy but successful lawyer who brokers arrangements between kidnappers and the families of their victims. He wears expensive suits and speaks in a low, menacing voice, the kind of man you want around when you need his particular talents – except that you hope you never have need of them.

The finished film is a swirling tornado of stylish camera work and visual razzle-dazzle. But unlike a number of Scott's previous efforts, *Man on Fire* is not an exercise in style over substance. Washington's gut-wrenching performance and a smart script make the film mesmerising from start to finish.

Made on a budget of $70 million and released in April 2004, *Man on Fire* would go on to gross well over $140 million worldwide, with another $30 million in home video revenues. Mickey Rourke had contributed to another huge hit.

Around this time, Rourke got another call from one of his new favourite directors. Robert Rodriguez was putting together a project that would be even further out there than *Once Upon a Time in Mexico*. He was wondering if Mickey would like a look at the screenplay. It was called *Sin City*.

Based on a comic book from which individual stories had been collated into many graphic novels, *Sin City* is a neo-*noir* nightmare that takes place in a filth and crime-filled metropolis where everything is for sale and everyone at risk. The original graphic novels were by the renowned writer and artist Frank Miller. Miller had had some bad experiences with Hollywood types, having written one of the *Robocop* screenplays and a few drafts of what was intended to be a resurrection of the *Batman* series. The duplicity and disloyalty surrounding his Hollywood experiences led him to declare he would never again sell his work to the movie industry. That went especially for the *Sin City* stories that had long been sought by young filmmakers for adaptation.

Rodriguez, a major comic book aficionado and Frank Miller fan, kept after Miller to sell him the rights to *Sin City*. Miller held firm. So Rodriguez took the unprecedented step of going ahead and shooting footage of what would become the opening sequence, as a way of auditioning for Miller. He used his high-tech studios in Austin to put the sequence together, as a way of showing his sincerity, and that he was operating with almost complete autonomy outside of the Hollywood system. And Rodriguez also had another ace up his sleeve. He was willing to offer Miller the job of co-directing the film with him, as a way of further guaranteeing he was not going to get fucked over again.

If Miller was impressed with the lengths Rodriguez was willing to go to win his support, he was blown away by the footage he was shown. When Rodriguez offered him the co-directing gig, Miller immediately embraced the project and pre-production was underway.

Rodriguez would show his early test footage to actors he was approaching for the lead roles as a way of introducing them to the unique way the film was going to be put together. He was boldly venturing to shoot the entire film against a green screen in his studio, and simply digitally paint in the background locations afterwards. When it came time to cast the role of Marv, Michael Madsen was tested for the role first but seemed uncomfortable in it. It was then passed along to Rourke for consideration, who Rodriguez had already decided he wanted in the film. (Madsen would end up in the film as Bob, the crooked cop who shoots Bruce Willis's character.)

By this time, Rodriguez would say that he could only really envision one actor playing this role, and that was Mickey Rourke. But he wanted Frank Miller to meet him as well, so the three got together and chatted about the project, with Rourke given the script and the graphic novels to read. In just minutes Miller would scribble in his notebook, 'Mickey Rourke IS Marv!'

Rourke was excited to be a part of the project. 'I love working with Rodriguez,' he said. 'He is a really talented guy and he is willing to try anything. And because he does everything himself, everything in his own facilities, he can do whatever he wants without a lot of interference from a lot of assholes who aren't a fraction as talented as he is.'

Rourke discussed the character of Marv and the themes in the graphic novels with his psychotherapist. The therapist came to the same conclusion as Miller – that there was a lot of Mickey Rourke in the character of Marv, and that he would be able to play the hell out of the character because he understood him on a profound level. So Rourke stepped up to join a cast that included Benicio Del Toro, Clive Owen and Bruce Willis.

Rourke would have to play Marv under a weight of latex appliances to give him an exaggerated look of menace. As much as it might have hindered another actor, Rourke had of course done it once before with his role in *Johnny Handsome*. 'I thought he was a great guy,' said make-up artist Greg Nicotero. 'From purely a work perspective he did everything we needed him to do without ever complaining even slightly, he actually showed a great interest in the process. He would joke around about not enjoying having to sit around motionless for so long, but then who would actually enjoy doing something like that day in and day out?'

Once shooting began it went smoothly, with everyone involved being very excited about being a part of something so cutting edge. *Sin City* is set in the underbelly of a rotten place called Basin City, and interweaves a few *noir*-inspired stories about the lives of a set of very desperate characters. At the centre of the film is the hulking brute named Marv, who wakes up one morning beside a dead prostitute named Goldie. Goldie was the only woman who ever showed him any tenderness at all, and it made no difference to him that he was paying her for it. He cannot remember what happened to her, but feels comfortably certain he will be blamed for the murder. So he heads out into the night, to find out just what happened to Goldie and avenge her death.

Other stories involve an ex-photojournalist (Owen) who accidentally kills a hero cop, a burned-out cop (Willis) battling heart problems, not to mention the prospect of going to prison for something he didn't do, and the hunting down of a sadistic thrill killer (Elijah Wood). The film also features a slew of leatherclad women, as lethal as pit vipers, who protect part of the city – Rosario Dawson and Jessica Alba fill their roles perfectly.

Because Rodriguez was shooting on video, he could shoot hours and hours of footage cheaply. *Sin City*, the film, was based on several entries in *Sin City*, the graphic novel series – *The Yellow Bastard, The Big Fat Kill* and the revised *The Hard Good Bye* – with an eye towards a few sequels for the big screen, then a few more for possible direct-to-DVD presentation. It meant that a lot of stuff was shot out of sequence, with any one of several actors on the sound-stage at any given time.

Rourke had a long, violent fight scene with Elijah Wood, but scheduling saw to it that the two would never actually meet. Rourke's portion of the sequence was shot before Wood even arrived in Austin, and they would not meet until the film's premiere. When asked about the day-to-day working atmosphere on the film, Rourke said, 'I would go on that set and it would be like fucking NASA in there. There was a green screen and all these computers all over the place.' But, as strange as the experience was, he knew he was surrounded by talented people who were all going for the same thing. 'He [Rodriguez] would go off for lunch and write some dialogue, dialogue that most guys in Hollywood couldn't come up with in a week if they tried,' said Rourke. 'I mean you can't help but love a guy who walks around the set in a Stetson strumming a Fender guitar telling you exactly what he needs while strumming a tune that he just wrote for the movie.'

*Sin City*, while violently over the top, was also a startlingly original piece of work. What Rodriguez and Miller (and 'guest director' Tarantino, who directed one of the story segments) showed was that you can have a film that is completely effects driven without compromising the story and the characters. For the actors, the film was an exercise in pure cinema. They were acting only to each other, or sometimes to nothing at all. 'It was like doing improv or experimental theatre,' said Owen. 'No, let me qualify that, it *was* doing improv and experimental theatre.'

Rourke enjoyed the atmosphere of being away from Hollywood, hanging out with the guys in Austin. 'The thing about this place is that you can live, you can just live here and be yourself,' he said. 'In LA everyone is out to hustle you, lie to you, fuck with you – the women are all fake boobed and looking for acting jobs and the men, or what passes for men out there, are all looking for whatever opportunity to sell out they can find. Down here you can do good work and live a normal life at the same time.' Rourke would go on to wildly proclaim, 'I am thinking seriously about moving down here to Austin, just as soon as my house lease runs out, I'm coming down here.'

As with the graphic novels, the imposing character of Marv is the most compelling in the film. He is a hulk with feelings and sensitivities that he is forced to keep bottled up inside him. Very tough and fearless, seemingly impervious to physical pain, he feels emotional pain deeply. All his violent actions are directed and determined by his emotional response to the loss of the only woman to show him tenderness. Rourke shone brightly in this role, and it certainly cemented his resurrected status.

The budget of $40 million may seem high for a film made on the fly. But the reality of the new digital Hollywood is that computers and technology don't make things easier, or cheaper, but they make things possible. And the film would be a major success. Released domestically on 1 April 2005, it pulled in almost $24 million during its opening weekend and went on to make over

*'Mickey Rourke IS Marv,' noted Frank Miller on seeing the actor audition for his* Sin City *(2005). The sensitive hulk returns in the first sequel of the new series franchise.*

$75 million during its domestic theatrical run, with another $40 million from foreign territories. The DVD release of the film was a source of great anticipation, as the trailblazing Rodriguez recut the film completely and expanded each storyline. There is a lot more material with Marv that is fascinating to watch – including a wonderful scene in which the fugitive goes to his childhood home and visits his mother, deepening the emotional content.

Rourke was now on a roll, hopscotching between projects with directors Robert Rodriguez and Tony Scott. But his next film with Scott almost didn't happen, although, once again, loyalty would win the day and bring it all together.

Domino Harvey was the daughter of famed actor Laurence Harvey (*The Manchurian Candidate*, *The Alamo*). She led the anchorless life of a child of the idle rich in Beverly Hills, before her life took a rather abrupt turn. For she ended up working as a bounty hunter for a while in Los Angeles, and all indications are that she was pretty proficient at it. Her story was of obvious interest to filmmakers, but Domino died of a suspicious drug overdose before the biopic of her life was released. When previously asked about the film, she was quoted as saying, 'If you are wondering what is true and what isn't, you can fuck off and mind your own business.'

When Rourke was offered *Domino*, he rejected it rather casually. 'I fucking hated it when I first read it,' he said. 'It read like exactly the kind of fucking movie that chased me from the business in the first place.' Not only that, but he was already committed to the Guy Ritchie film *Revolver*, in England. For Ritchie and Rourke had conducted a mutual admiration society from a distance – both admired the other's work very much, and had hoped to work together. 'I was actually on my way to London to do the Ritchie film,' said Rourke. 'Then Tony Scott calls me up and says that he wants me to do this film with him. I was not really responding immediately to the material. But Tony was a guy who reached out and gave me a chance, who showed great confidence in me when I needed it, so we have some history there and I wanted to honour that.'

Scott listened patiently to Rourke's objections, but none of his arguments changed the fact that it was he Scott had in mind for the role of Ed Moseby. Rourke told him that he thought the role lacked any dimensions, and that virtually any actor in Hollywood could play the part as well or better than he could. 'It seems like the guys who wrote this have never left the tennis court and have certainly never met guys like the guys they were writing about,' he observed. This is something Rourke had over the writers – he *had* met guys like these, often. 'Yeah, you see these guys around the bike shows or at the fights or at the gym, there is no set type. Bounty hunters can look like anyone or anything, that is how they are able to do what they do.'

Scott asked Rourke what he would do differently if he were the one creating the character. Rourke told him he would be interested in playing Moseby as a tough guy with a past, who did not grow up wanting to be a bounty hunter, but got caught in a life that funnelled down to him after he'd exhausted all the rest of his options. Scott told Rourke that if he would agree to do the film, he could play Moseby however he saw fit. Rourke dropped out of the Guy Ritchie film and signed on with Scott – something that Ritchie obviously forgave him for, as Rourke would attend the London premiere of *Revolver*.

Every actor with a sustained career has projects they turned down that they probably should have taken, and films they did take that they probably should have passed on. Mickey Rourke is no different. Dustin Hoffman badly wanted him to play the role ultimately filled by Tom Cruise in *Rain Man*. Rourke never responded to the script because he was too preoccupied at the time to even read it. He also turned down the Cruise role in *Top Gun*, while *The Untouchables*, *Highlander* and *48 Hours* were all sent his way. So it was when he turned down *Revolver* in favour of *Domino*.

In the film, Domino Harvey is played by rising young star Keira Knightley (*Bend It Like Beckham, Pirates of the Caribbean*), and she does her best to play tough and look the part. But ultimately she is never really convincing, and her notices were particularly brutal. (She was reportedly reduced to tears by one negative piece.) Rourke fully embodies his role as Domino's boss – he looks tough and grizzled, but the general feeling about his layered performance is that it was lost in the overstylised visuals, and the whittling down of the story to its lowest possible common denominator. Mexican actor Edgar Ramirez also does his best as the third bounty hunter, named Choko, but even his charisma could not pull his performance out of the film's swirling silliness. But Ramirez has an intensity and an ability to play animal instincts naturally on screen, so he comes off as the best of the three leads.

Whatever the quality of the film, Rourke did get along well with Keira Knightley. He was asked, during the shooting, if he was giving her advice on how to avoid the potholes on the road he had already travelled. 'No, not really,' said Rourke. 'Let me tell you something, I would be sitting in the make-up trailer and I'd look at her and she'd be reading her third book in two weeks. There was nothing I could tell this girl. She knows what time it is. I met her mom and I can see why she is the way that she is. She's very intelligent. She's a real lady. She's not one of these Hollywood cunts. I have a lot of respect for her as a person.'

*Domino* is a noisy, senselessly violent, ridiculously profane movie that goes nowhere and gets there very fast. The writing is cheap and tawdry. Every other word of dialogue is 'fuck' – *fuck off! fuck you! get the fuck outta here! drop your fucking weapon, motherfucker!* – and 'Muthafucka' is actually the title of one of the songs on the soundtrack. The argument is always that this is the way such people speak in real life. But this isn't real life, it's a movie, and they aren't real people, they are written characters. What Scott did here – and it's almost diametrically opposed to what he did with *Man on Fire* – was take a compelling story and turn it into a fast-cutting, rap-soundtracked, loud, angry mess aimed clearly at the average MTV viewer.

Budgeted at about $50 million, *Domino* was justly considered a flop. Its opening weekend grossed only $4 million, with its domestic theatrical run only bringing in $11 million. It did far better overseas, bringing in just over $20 million, but still didn't come even close to profitability.

Domino Harvey fully co-operated with the project, and is honourably paid tribute at the end of the film. Rourke grew fond of her, as they'd spent some time together on the set. When she died, he was deeply saddened. Just before her death, Rourke had checked into the hospital to have his appendix removed. Even though he had just gone through the surgical procedure, he insisted on joining Tony Scott, who read a heartfelt eulogy to the gathering of mourners. 'I could barely fucking stand up I was so woozy,' said Rourke. 'But nothing was going to keep me from being there to see her off.'

After Rourke finished *Domino* he headed to England, where he had accepted a small role in a film aimed at younger audiences called *Stormbreaker*. The film is based on the first of a series of novels aimed at younger readers by Anthony Horowitz, concerning a reluctant fourteen-year-old hero pressed into service by the Special Operations Division of Britain's ultra-secret intelligence agency, MI6. These books, known as the Alex Ryder series, have sold close to ten million copies worldwide and have been translated into over twenty languages.

Rourke plays a character called Darrius Sayle, a strange billionaire in whose hands the fates of billions rest. Decked out in oddly coloured clothes and shoulder-length red hair with a goatee, his back story is that he was bullied by the future Prime Minister of Britain when they attended the same boarding school. He plans a twisted revenge on millions of schoolchildren the world over, by giving them all his new Stormbreaker computers with a deadly virus built into them. This impressive looking film also features Ewan McGregor and Alicia Silverstone.

After shooting a small role in a film with big potential, Rourke headed to Toronto to get back on the comeback train. His choice of *Killshot* for his next role, based on the novel by Elmore Leonard, may just prove to be the shrewdest move he and his agent have made yet.

*Killshot* had been in development for a number of years. Author Leonard told me, as far back as the summer of 2000, that it was one of five of his novels under option to Quentin Tarantino and his production company, A Band Apart. The plan was for Tarantino to direct a few of the films and produce the rest. *Killshot* will now be executive produced by Tarantino alongside the Weinstein brothers, for their new venture called the Weinstein Company.

As a Canadian who has lived his life in Toronto, I was surprised that Leonard chose to begin his novel with a long segment set in a seedy section of my city. The main character, a Native American hitman named Armand 'Black Bird' Degas, is living in an actual Toronto dive called the Spadina Hotel. I asked Leonard about this when I interviewed him for a magazine profile. 'I called a friend of mine up there in Toronto and asked him where a guy like Degas would live in that town,' he said. 'He told me the Spandina Hotel, and that was that. Research doesn't have to be all complicated, you know.'

*Killshot* is like virtually all Leonard's crime novels – rich in detail, and written in such a way that you not only picture what he is describing with ease, you also hear the voices of the characters just as clearly. His Armand Degas is a guy who just wants to be left alone, to live his life and get as many small pleasures out of it as he can. He is not greedy and he is not ambitious. He just is what he is. A hitman. I called Leonard to ask him about his reaction to casting Mickey Rourke in the Degas role. 'I like it, I like it a lot,' he said. 'He is a fantastic actor and he is perfect for portraying the quiet intensity and lurking menace of Degas, while at the same time being able to sell his simplicity.'

The *Killshot* screenplay was written by Hossein Amini (*The Four Feathers*) and Steve Barancik, who was last credited with the storyline for Rourke's previous film, *Domino*. It's understandably not as layered and detailed as the novel, rounding off the edges of Leonard's story of the Native American hitman who goes to Detroit to bump off a high ranking mobster, only to become inadvertently involved with some lowlife criminals who don't realise how dangerous he is. The character that survives the most intact is Rourke's Armand Degas. The location shoot in Toronto (with a bit of location shooting in Cape Giradeau, Missouri) had less to do with the opening passages of the book than with tax incentives and the relatively weak US/Canadian dollar exchange.

John Madden directed the film. Having scored big with *Shakespeare in Love*, though he stumbled a little with *Captain Corelli's Mandolin* and *Proof,* he infuses it with a nice measure of grit played against style. He also has a terrific cast that includes Diane Lane, Thomas Jane and Rourke's *Sin City* co-star, Rosario Dawson. (Johnny Knoxville is also in the film, but he's the weakest link. He's a clown, not an actor.)

Those who worked on the Toronto set of *Killshot* reported that Mickey Rourke was courteous, cooperative and always on time. But he enjoyed his off-hours in the city. He had dinner at his favourite Italian joint, Cafe Vaticano (where he has a particular fondness for the spaghetti bolognese), with ex-Canadian boxing champ George Chuvallo. Chuvallo entertained the enrapt Rourke with stories of his epic Toronto fight in 1966 against Muhammad Ali (then known as Cassius Clay). Chuvallo has the distinction of having gone toe to toe with Ali for fifteen rounds without being knocked down, but lost on decision. Rourke also stopped by the tattoo parlour/merchandise store of the Toronto chapter of the Hells Angels, where he picked up a sweatshirt. ('I can take any kind of heat, but I cannot fucking stand the cold,' said Rourke, during the chilly, rainy October of 2005.) He took in the strange trade fair known as the Everything To Do About Sex Show, where he checked out the X-rated video booth manned by his pal, famed porn star Ron Jeremy, and also spent some time with his old Actor's Studio pal, Christopher Walken, who was working in Toronto on a different movie.

After shooting *Killshot* in Toronto, Rourke went directly into prep work for two other films. The first, *The Night Job*, is scheduled to be directed by John McNaughton, infamous for making the

*The three bounty hunters in* Domino *(2005) – right to left: Domino Harvey (Keira Knightley), Ed Moseby (Mickey Rourke), and Choko (Edgar Ramirez).*

seriously creepy *Henry: Portrait of a Serial Killer.* The film is to star Rourke, Ray Liotta, Marisa Tomei, Robin Wright Penn and WWE wrestler Darren Matthews. Michael Mailer, the eldest son of legendary writer Norman Mailer, is the producer.

From there, Rourke will go right into the much-anticipated sequel to *Sin City. Sin City 2* will again be shot at the Troublemaker Studios in Austin, Texas. It will pick up where the original film left off, with the character of Dwight (Clive Owen) contemplating all the wrongheaded decisions and mistakes he has made, and how he is going to undo them. There is also a side story involving the character of Nancy (Jessica Alba) dealing with the death of Hartigan (Bruce Willis). When asked about playing the role of Marv again, Rourke said, 'Are you kidding, I loved playing that guy and I loved being around those filmmakers, if they want me to do seven more of those films I would be more than happy to say yes to that.' Which appears to be exactly the plan that Robert Rodriguez and Frank Miller have for the budding *Sin City* franchise.

And it seems Rodriguez will still not be finished with Mickey Rourke quite yet. His name has been connected to another quirky little Rodriguez/Tarantino collaboration, a mini-double feature horror presentation paying tribute to the old double features of the Fifties, Sixties and Seventies, called *Grind House.* The plan is for Rodriguez and Tarantino to direct a 75-minute feature each – Tarantino will make *Death Proof*, a slasher film, while Rodriguez will make *Perfect Terror*, a more Hitchcockian offering. They will also both direct a couple of mock trailers for the intermission. Besides Rourke, the cast so far includes Michael Biehn, Tom Savini and Danny Trejo. But early word from the production office indicates that Mickey Rourke may not end up playing the character called Stunt Man Mike at all. It seems there has been a conflict, either creative or scheduling, that might just see Mickey Rourke replaced by Kurt Russell.

Rourke has also been developing a film project with Ice-T, a Western about a bounty hunter and a slave who runs away to join the Union Army, so he can hunt down the Confederate soldiers who tortured him.

Out of curiosity, I asked Rourke during our interview if there was a filmmaker he was still anxious to work with. 'I would love to do something with Oliver Stone,' he said without any hesitation at all. 'We get together for dinner or conversations pretty frequently, so I am sure that the chance of actually doing something in the way of work together will happen sooner rather than later.'

This reminded me of something else I wanted to ask. 'Is it true that you were actually offered the role of Barnes in Stone's breakout film *Platoon*?' 'Yeah, we talked about that around the time that we were working on *Year of the Dragon*,' said Rourke. 'But the *Platoon* that I was offered, the script that I read, was not the *Platoon* that Oliver ended up making, which I loved. The *Platoon* I read had a murder theme to it, it was more of an action movie than the fantastic film about men and war that he ended up making.'

What Mickey Rourke needed to effect his comeback was a solid hit, and to play a significant role in its success. It happened with *Sin City*. Now it is up to him. 'I know this is it,' said Rourke. 'I have no more chances left. If I fuck this up this time, there will not be a next time and I live with that deep belief every day. And because I know that, and because I know where some of the decisions I made in the past put me, I know how fucking lucky I am that I even have this second go at it. So, believe me, I ain't looking to fuck up anymore.'

Most people hear the name Mickey Rourke and immediately associate it with a rebellious, badboy image. Then they think of the films, and his performances, afterwards. What you may have noticed in these pages is that there is very little discussion of his bad-boy behaviour, because, frankly, there was very little evidence of it to be found. One photographer who was assigned the job of shooting pictures of Rourke, for the now defunct LA style magazine *Bikini*, said he was nervous about the assignment, only to find that his subject was a softly spoken, generous person. And this was a description I came across time and time again. The commonly believed tabloid version of the Mickey Rourke story is pure Hollywood – more legend and fable than truth.

The demons that overtook Rourke during his first incarnation as a movie star have been identified, and wrestled into submission. The interesting work is starting to flow his way again, and he is responding to the material appropriately. His story proves that you can be an individual, and remain stoically committed to that individuality, and still get a second chance if you've blown it first time around. Sometimes, people want to root for the guy who is getting up after being knocked on his ass.

Mickey Rourke's somewhat cautionary tale is still unfolding, but he is already assured of a place, and a certain notoriety, in the history of modern cinema.

# FILMOGRAPHY

**1941** (1979)
Directed By Steven Spielberg
Starring John Belushi, Dan
Aykroyd, Treat Williams (with
Mickey Rourke as Private
Reese)

**CITY IN FEAR** (1980)
Directed by Jud Taylor (as Alan
Smithee)
Starring David Janssen, Robert
Vaughn (with Mickey Rourke as
Tony Pate)

**ACT OF LOVE** (1980)
Directed by Jud Taylor
Starring Ron Howard, Robert
Foxworth (with Mickey Rourke
as Joseph Cybulkowski)

**FADE TO BLACK** (1980)
Directed by Vernon Zimmerman
Starring Dennis Christopher, Tim
Thomerson (with Mickey Rourke
as Ritchie)

**RAPE AND MARRIAGE: THE
RIDEOUT CASE** (1980)
Directed by Peter Levin
Starring Mickey Rourke (as John
Rideout), Linda Hamilton, Rip Torn

**MICHAEL CIMINO'S HEAVEN'S
GATE** (1980)
Directed by Michael Cimino
Starring Kris Kristofferson,
Christopher Walken, Isabelle
Huppert (with Mickey Rourke as
Nick Ray)

**BODY HEAT** (1981)
Directed by Lawrence Kasdan
Starring William Hurt, Kathleen
Turner (with Mickey Rourke as
Teddy Lewis)

**DINER** (1982)
Directed by Barry Levinson
Starring Mickey Rourke (as Boo-
gie), Kevin Bacon, Daniel Stern,
Ellen Barkin

**RUMBLE FISH** (1983)
Directed by Francis Ford Coppola
Starring Matt Dillon, Diane Lane,
Nicolas Cage, Dennis Hopper,
Mickey Rourke (as the Motorcycle
Boy)

**THE POPE OF GREENWICH
VILLAGE** (1984)
Directed by Stuart Rosenberg
Starring Mickey Rourke (as
Charlie Moran), Eric Roberts,
Daryl Hannah, Geraldine
Fitzgerald

**YEAR OF THE DRAGON** (1985)
Directed by Michael Cimino
Starring Mickey Rourke (as Stan-
ley White), John Lone, Arianne

**NINE AND A HALF WEEKS**
(1986)
Directed by Adrian Lyne
Starring Mickey Rourke (as
John), Kim Basinger, Margaret
Whitton

**ANGEL HEART** (1987)
Directed by Alan Parker
Starring Mickey Rourke (as
Harold Angel), Robert De Niro,
Lisa Bonet, Charlotte Rampling

**A PRAYER FOR THE DYING**
(1987)
Directed by Mike Hodges
Starring Mickey Rourke (as
Martin Fallon), Alan Bates, Bob
Hoskins

**BARFLY** (1987)
Directed by Barbet Schroeder
Starring Mickey Rourke (as
Henry Chinaski), Faye Dunaway,
Alice Krige

**HOMEBOY** (1988)
Directed by Michael Seresin
Starring Mickey Rourke (as
Johnny Walker), Christopher
Walken, Debra Feuer

**FRANCESCO** (1989)
Directed by Liliana Cavani
Starring Mickey Rourke (as
Francis of Assisi), Helena Bon-
ham Carter, Mario Adorf

**JOHNNY HANDSOME** (1989)
Directed by Walter Hill
Starring Mickey Rourke (as John
Sedley), Morgan Freeman, Forest
Whitaker, Ellen Barkin

**WILD ORCHID** (1990)
Directed by Zalman King
Starring Mickey Rourke (as
James Wheeler), Carre Otis,
Bruce Greenwood, Jacqueline
Bisset

**DESPERATE HOURS** (1990)
Directed by Michael Cimino
Starring Mickey Rourke (as
Michael Bosworth), Anthony
Hopkins, Mimi Rogers, Elias
Koteas

**HARLEY DAVIDSON AND THE
MARLBORO MAN** (1991)
Directed by Simon Wincer
Starring Mickey Rourke (as
Harley), Don Johnson, Chelsea
Field

**WHITE SANDS** (1992)
Directed by Roger Donaldson
Starring Willem Dafoe, Mary
Elizabeth Mastrantonio, Mickey
Rourke (as Gorman Lennox)

**F.T.W.** (1994)
Directed by Michael Karbelnikoff
Starring Mickey Rourke (as
Frank T. Wells), Aaron Neville,
Lori Singer

**THE LAST OUTLAW** (1994)
Directed by Geoff Murphy
Starring Mickey Rourke (as
Graff), Dermott Mulroney, Steve
Buscemi

**FALL TIME** (1995)
Directed by Paul Warner
Starring Stephen Baldwin, David
Arquette, Mickey Rourke (as
Florence)

**EXIT IN RED** (1996)
Directed by Yurek Bogayevicz
Starring Mickey Rourke (as Ed
Altman), Anthony Michael Hall,
Carre Otis

**BULLET (1996)**
Directed by Julien Temple
Starring Mickey Rourke (as
Butch), Adrien Brody, Tupac
Shakur, Ted Levine

**DOUBLE TEAM** (1996)
Directed by Tsui Hark
Starring Mickey Rourke (as
Stavros), Jean Claude Van
Damme, Dennis Rodman

**LOVE IN PARIS** (1997)
Directed by Anne Goursaud
Starring Mickey Rourke (as John
Gray), Angie Everhardt, Dougray
Scott

**THE RAINMAKER** (1997)
Directed by Francis Ford Coppola

Starring Matt Damon, Danny
DeVito, Clare Danes, Mickey
Rourke (as Bruiser Stone)

**BUFFALO 66** (1998)
Directed by Vincent Gallo
Starring Vincent Gallo, Christina
Ricci, Mickey Rourke (as the
Bookie)

**THICKER THAN BLOOD** (1998)
Directed by Richard Pearce
Starring Mickey Rourke (as
Father Frank Larkin), Dan Futter-
man, Carlos Alban

**THURSDAY** (1998)
Directed by Skip Woods
Starring Thomas Jane, Paulina
Poriskova, Mickey Rourke (as
Khasarov)

**POINT BLANK** (1998)
Directed by Max Earl Beesley
Starring Werner Schreyer, Danny
Trejo, Mickey Rourke (as Rudy
Ray)

**THE THIN RED LINE** (1998)
Directed by Terrence Malick
Starring Sean Penn, Jim
Caviezel, Nick Nolte (Mickey
Rourke as a soldier was edited
from the film)

**SHERGAR** (1999)
Directed by Dennis Lewiston
Starring Alan Barker, Billy Boyer,
Mickey Rourke (as Gavin
O'Rourke)

**OUT IN FIFTY** (1999)
Directed by Bojesse Christopher
Starring Christina Applegate,
Alexis Arquette, Mickey Rourke
(as Bracken)

**SHADES** (1999)
Directed by Erik Van Looy
Starring Gene Bervoets, Peter

Borghs, Mickey Rourke (as Paul
Sullivan)

**ANIMAL FACTORY** (2000,
released 2002)
Directed by Steve Buscemi
Starring Willem Dafoe, Edward
Furlong, Mickey Rourke (as Jan
the Actress)

**GET CARTER** (2000)
Directed by Stephen Kay
Starring Sylvester Stallone, Alan
Cumming, Mickey Rourke (as
Cyrus Paice)

**THEY CRAWL** (2001)
Directed by John Allardice
Starring Daniel Cosgrove, Tama-
ra Davies, Mickey Rourke (as
Tiny Frakes)

**THE PLEDGE** (2001)
Directed by Sean Penn
Starring Jack Nicholson, Robin
Wright Penn, Mickey Rourke (as
Jim Olstad)

**THE HIRE – THE FOLLOW**
(2001)
Directed by Wong Kar-Wai
Starring Clive Owen, Adrianna
Lima, Mickey Rourke (as the
Husband)

**PICTURE CLAIRE** (2001)
Directed by Bruce McDonald
Starring Juliette Lewis, Callum
Keith Rennie, Mickey Rourke (as
Eddie)

**SPUN** (2002)
Directed by Jonas Akerlund
Starring Jason Schwartzman,
Brittany Murphy, Eric Roberts,
Mickey Rourke (as the Cook)

**MASKED AND ANONYMOUS**
(2003)
Directed by Larry Charles

Starring Bob Dylan, Jeff Bridges, Val Kilmer, Mickey Rourke (as Edmund)

## ONCE UPON A TIME IN MEXICO (2003)
Directed by Robert Rodriguez
Starring Antonio Banderas, Selma Hayek, Johnny Depp, Mickey Rourke (as Billy Chambers)

## MAN ON FIRE (2004)
Directed by Tony Scott
Starring Denzel Washington, Dakota Fanning, Mark Anthony, Christopher Walken, Mickey Rourke (as Jordan)

## DRIV3R (2004)
Directed by Maurice Suckling
Starring (voices only) Michael Madsen, Ving Rhames, Mickey Rourke (as Jericho)

## SIN CITY (2005)
Directed by Robert Rodriguez/Frank Miller
Starring Clive Owen, Bruce Willis, Jessica Alba, Mickey Rourke (as Marv)

## DOMINO (2005)
Directed by Tony Scott
Starring Keira Knightley, Edgar Ramirez, Mickey Rourke (as Ed Moseby)

## TRUE CRIME – NEW YORK CITY (2005)
Directed by Matthew Cirrulnik
Starring (voices only) Laurence Fishburne, Christopher Walken, Mickey Rourke (as Terrence Higgins)

## STORMBREAKER (2006)
Directed by Geoffrey Sax
Starring Ewan McGregor, Alex Pettyfer, Mickey Rourke (as Darrius Sayle)

## KILLSHOT (2006)
Directed by John Madden
Starring Diane Lane, Thomas Jane, Mickey Rourke (as Armand Degas)

## THE NIGHT JOB (2006)
Directed by John McNaughton
Starring Ray Liotta, Marisa Tomei, Mickey Rourke (as Boots)

## SIN CITY 2 (2007)
Directed by Robert Rodriguez/Frank Miller
Starring Clive Owen, Jessica Alba, Mickey Rourke (as Marv)

## GRIND HOUSE (2007)
Directed by Robert Rodriguez/Quentin Tarantino
Starring Michael Biehn, Tom Savini, Danny Trejo
Mickey Rourke (tentative)